The Best
Men's Stage Monologues
of 1998

Other books by Jocelyn A. Beard

Smith and Kraus *Books For Actors*
THE MONOLOGUE SERIES

The Best Men's / Women's Stage Monologues of 1997
The Best Men's / Women's Stage Monologues of 1996
The Best Men's / Women's Stage Monologues of 1995
The Best Men's / Women's Stage Monologues of 1994
The Best Men's / Women's Stage Monologues of 1993
The Best Men's / Women's Stage Monologues of 1992
The Best Men's / Women's Stage Monologues of 1991
The Best Men's / Women's Stage Monologues of 1990
One Hundred Men's / Women's Stage Monologues from the 1980s
2 Minutes and Under: Character Monologues for Actors
Street Talk: Character Monologues for Actors
Uptown: Character Monologues for Actors
Ice Babies in Oz: Character Monologues for Actors
Monologues from Contemporary Literature: Volume I
Monologues from Classic Plays
100 Great Monologues from the Renaissance Theatre
100 Great Monologues from the Neo-Classical Theatre
100 Great Monologues from the 19th C. Romantic and Realistic Theatre
A Brave and Violent Theatre: 20th C. Irish Monologues, Scenes & Hist. Context
Kiss and Tell: Restoration Monologues, Scenes and Historical Context
The Great Monologues from the Humana Festival
The Great Monologues from the EST Marathon
The Great Monologues from the Women's Project
The Great Monologues from the Mark Taper Forum

YOUNG ACTOR SERIES

Great Scenes and Monologues for Children
Great Monologues for Young Actors
Multicultural Monologues for Young Actors

SCENE STUDY SERIES

Scenes From Classic Plays 468 B.C. to 1960 A.D.
The Best Stage Scenes of 1998
The Best Stage Scenes of 1997
The Best Stage Scenes of 1996
The Best Stage Scenes of 1995
The Best Stage Scenes of 1994
The Best Stage Scenes of 1993
The Best Stage Scenes of 1992
The Best Stage Scenes for Men / Women from the 1980s

If you require pre-publication information about upcoming Smith and Kraus books, you may receive our semi-annual catalogue, free of charge, by sending your name and address to *Smith and Kraus Catalogue, 4 Lower Mill Road, North Stratford, NH 03590. Or call us at (800) 895-4331, fax (603) 922-3348.*

The Best
Men's Stage Monologues
of 1998

edited by Jocelyn A. Beard

The Monologue Audition Series

SK
A Smith and Kraus Book

Published by Smith and Kraus, Inc.
One Main Street, Lyme, NH 03768

First Edition: September1999
10 9 8 7 6 5 4 3 2 1

The Monologue Audition Series ISSN 1067-134X

NOTE: These monologues are intended to be used for audition and class study; permission is not required to use the material for those purposes. However, if there is a paid performance of any of the monologues included in this book, please refer to the permissions acknowledgment pages to locate the source who can grant permission for public performance.

Contents

Preface

Theatre is dead! You just can't open an upmarket periodical these days without being dragged into a panel discussion on theatre's oft reported demise. Critics like John Simon and his cronies pass "Theatre is Dead" from lip to lip making it a gloomy and somewhat tiresome mantra that they would very much like us all to share. Misery loves company, you know. What non-sense.

As Victor Frankenstein once so eloquently declared: "It's alive!" So alive, in fact, that actors now find themselves in a unique time and place in which so much more is required than the ability to emote like you're in a heavy scene on "NYPD Blue."

Playwrights and directors are going crazy with all sorts of wild staging. Puppets, commedia d'el arte and broad physicality are all making delightful returns to the stage. Since I've misquoted Mary Shelley I may as well go for the gold and quote Mr. Homer Simpson: "Woo-hoo!"

A delectable crop of fresh material was offered up in 1998. Those of you seeking that 'ole bare bones emotional drama should check out monologues from *Killer Joe,* and *The Dying Gaul.* Wild and crazy guys looking for stuff that's definitely on the edge should take a gander at *Armagideon, Poona the Fuckdog,* and *Sakina's Restaurant.* The under twenty crowd will find cool material in *The Dead Boy,* and *'Til the Rapture Comes.* Those of you who are satisfied only with characters who are larger than life will find them. Get ready for George Wallace in *Cornelia;* Cesare Borgia in *Evil Legacy,* Agamemnon in *Agamemnon* and Othello's nemesis, Iago in *What More?* Funny guys should look to the comedic offerings of *Freak, Dating Dummies, Prelude to Pizza,* and *Seven Dates with Seven Writers.*

Remember, if you find something you like...READ THE PLAY!

Break a Leg!
Jocelyn Beard
The Brickhouse
(One Hot) Summer 1999

This book is dedicated with love to
Karen Dapper, Barbara Harris, and Joanne Oxx
for providing me with the essentials:
space, food, and laughter.

Agamemnon

Andrew C. Ordover

From the Atreides Plays of Aeschylus and Euripides

Scene: the palace of Agamemnon

Dramatic
Agamemnon: doomed king returned from war. 40s–50s

> *Agamemnon has returned from battle to find himself ill-at-ease with his wife, Clytemnestra. Here, he tries to explain to her why he is no longer the same man that she sent off to battle.*

AGAMEMNON: A year ago
A year before the end
The Trojans took to cutting off
The heads of those they killed
They kept them up on pikes
And threw them down on us
Whenever we approached
The faces of our friends

Like bombs upon us   .
Raining down
The dead eyes staring
Blue tongues slapping rubber cheeks
A year ago
And every day since then

The things
You cannot know
Unwordable but
Necessary
Things

I had to do
To conquer such a will
To smash that wall and

Win

Loving men
You understand
All decent men
To do those things
And worse
And worse

I'm not the man you knew

Armagideon

Sandra Dempsey

Scene: a house at the end of the world

Dramatic
Nathan: a man torn apart by desire in the face of global destruction. 20–30

> *The world is on the absolute brink of a major nuclear war and Nathan has returned to the only home he has ever known which is now ground zero. Realizing that the nukes are about to fly, Nathan paces wildly in the small house spouting military techno-speak in a failed attempt to keep from going mad.*

NATHAN: 'Better to die than be a coward. 'Better to *die.*

First Enemy of Survival: Pain! If you give in to it, it'll weaken your *drive to survive!* Don't try to relieve the pain of others—always look out for yourself, *first* and always *first!*

Alpha, Beta, Gamma!

Second Enemy of Survival: Cold! Cold is insidious—it numbs the mind and the body and the will.

Third Enemy: Thirst! It'll dull your mind. Serious dehydration can occur with exposure to *radiation enhancement devices,* even when there's *plenty* of water! Be *ruthless!* Save *thyself! Shared* water is *less* water!

Fourth Enemy of Survival: Hunger! 'Lessons ability for rational thinking! 'Increases susceptibility to the weaknesses caused by *cold, pain,* and *fear!*

It is better to die—and eye—and slip the surly bondage—and *sit on your face!*

(He is losing control. He is ravenous for sensation, fighting the feel of his own flesh. He is stripped down to his undershorts.)

Fatigue! 'Makes you careless—reduces mental ability! Fatigue represents an *escape*—hopelessness

Boredom and Loneliness! Two of the toughest Enemies of Survival!

Darkness will elevate your level of fear by a factor of six!

Survival Readiness Phase—Warning Phase—Threat Phase Pre-Attack Phase—

Attack-period!

Response Phase—Rescue Phase—Recovery Phase—Reconstruction Phase...doesn't *faze* me!

Airborne Vectors, eroding the *will of the population...*

My Radiation Enhancement Device is an efficient nuclear weapon that eliminates your enemy with minimum damage to *friendly* territory! It's a *neutron cookie-cutter!* It'll kill people inside a three-quarter-mile radius *without harming soldiers nearby!* It works by attacking the central nervous system—the body convulses, limbs shake, the nervous system fails, so that all of the automatic body functions, *even breathing,* are affected—death comes within forty-eight hours from respiratory failure or swelling of tissues in the brain!

(Almost dream-like.) Irradiated Fuel Rods leaking weapons grade plutonium...

(Frantic.) Wanted: Enlisted personnel to work on nuclear fissionable isotope molecular reactive counters and phase cyclotronic uranium and plutonium photo synthesizers. No experience necessary!

(He mimics and vocalizes the following warning signals.)

Brrrrrriiiinnnnggg! Ringing bell and flashing red light: high airborne radioactivity! Evacuate area!

Wwwwweeehhhaaaoooowwweeehhhaaaooo! Siren-wavering tone for three to six minutes: Take Cover! Stay Inside!

Wwwwwwwhhhhhhhheeeeeeeeeeeee! Siren—steady blast for three to six minutes: Evacuation! Go To Staging Area!

Gong-gong-gong-gong-gong-gong-gong! Atomic Fire: Evacuate!

Aahh-ooo-gah! Aahh-ooo-gah! Criticality! *Run!!*

(Panicking.) Run and tell—*BMEWS* your Ballistic Missile Early Warning Systems—and *COLOG* your Co-operative Logistics for a mandated emergency!

Push an *MFU* your Mobile Feeding Unit for mixed fission products and *always* trust in your Radiation Protection Survey and Computation *RAPSAC* for a chemical cloud dispersion in your Single Kill Probability and your World Wide Military Comrnand and Control System—and go tell it on the mountain Regional Operation Control Centre, go tell 'em about Mutual Assured Destruction…

(There is a tremendous thunder-clap. He collapses to the floor.)

(Quietly, miming his words.) He had a pistol with him and placed it to his forehead, apparently thinking he would never be found.

The Beach Club

Ludmilla Bollow

Scene: December 1. A Beach.

Serio-Comic
Jake: a lonely middle-aged man who sits on the beach every day from the first day of spring to the first day of winter. 50s

> *Jake will yack with anyone who will listen. In fact, he'll talk even if no one's listening. Here, he rambles on about the perils of winter.*

JAKE: Aagh, this puzzle's too dang hard today. *(Closes paper.)* You ain't too cold are you?

[Allegra doesn't answer.]

JAKE: I mean, you don't have no extra padding like me. *(Pause. Talks, but to no one in particular.)* You know, I must have bear instincts, cause when I see that first snow, smell it in the air even, I get this feeling inside me, to go hibernate in my room. I got this big old fur rug—curl up under it most of the day…Sometimes, I just lay there and eat peanuts. Buy a hundred pounds in fall. Shells all over the damn place. But, why bother. Wish I really was a bear, sleep the whole winter through.

[ALLEGRA: It would be nice to sleep away parts of our life we don't want to live through. Erase them all with sleep. *(Takes out bottle of pills. Stares at it.)*]

JAKE: Hate winters! Always have! Aagh, when I was a kid, my ma, she'd bundle me up so, could hardly walk. Long underwear, wool socks, snow pants—scarves all over my face. Couldn't even see. And those smelly flannel rags—dipped in hot rancid goose grease, pinned to my undershirt. Itched like hell. Vicks up my nose, pine and tar cough syrup down my throat—All winter long, couldn't breathe.

The Beach Club

Ludmilla Bollow

Serio-Comic
Jake: a lonely middle-aged man who sits on the beach every day from the first day of spring to the first day of winter. 50s

> *Here, Jake takes a moment to remember his father, a flag-pole sitter.*

JAKE: My dad, he was a flagpole sitter—

[SIGMUND: He was?]

JAKE: Yep. Sat on top that flagpole for thirty-one days. Nights too. Now that was really something to see. Crowds of people standing below, just waiting for him to give up. My ma, she stood there every day too, madder'n a wet hen, screaming at him to come down. Didn't pay no attention to her. Just sat there. Waiting out his thirty-one days.

Now there was a man what could endure things. Hell, sitting down here is nothing compared to him spending thirty-one days on top that tiny flagpole...Lots of times, gets pretty nippy down here, I think—what the hell, what am I proving anyways. Then, I start thinking bout my dad, sitting up there, never giving up. And you know what he said to me day he came down—he said, "Son, it was worth every minute of it. I finally did something spectacular in my life, and nobody can ever take it away from me!" Even on his deathbed, asked to see the clippings. And there was a smile on his face when he went, like his life wasn't wasted after all.

Blue Falls, Indiana

Nannette Stone

Scene: Blue Falls, Indiana

Dramatic
Paul: a teacher haunted by his past. 36.

> *When a student is raped, Paul is forced to confront powerful
> demons of guilt from his past. Here, he confesses all to his
> wife.*

PAUL: Sometimes the more you tell yourself a lie, the more it seems
true. But I can't lie to myself about this anymore.

The summer before our senior year in high school, Kit Bishop
and I worked at McDonald's. We started to talk after work. I
found out that she wrote poetry and that she planned to skip
town the day she graduated. Her tight clothes and that highway
sign yellow hair of hers made me think maybe I could touch her
in places half the other guys in school said they had. Maybe I
could have. But I didn't. She was smart and funny and—and
well—it was the way she always looked right into my eyes when
I talked to her—like she was really listening.

I started telling her stuff I hadn't told anyone. About getting
picked last in gym and about being short. Girls looming over me
in the halls. She said she felt lonely. That she was tired of being
herself and that someday she was going to be somebody important. Said "Who gives a damn if everyone thinks I sleep around?"
She even told me about her father.

Well September comes along and I can't believe I've grown
almost six inches taller. Got Dad's old Ford. Made the football
team. And all of a sudden I am right there. Sitting on Ben Baker's
porch. Drunk as a skunk, partying with Bill Allan and Tommy
Thompson. And Jim drives up with Kit in the car. He pulls her out.
She stumbles onto the grass and lies down on her back. Her eyes

are all smeared-black with mascara. She isn't wearing a bra and her sweater is unbuttoned down the front.

Come on Jim says and the guys start lining up. Jim has hiked up her skirt and is already on top of her and Bobby is next in line with his fly unzipped. Tommy goes next and then Bill. Come on they say to me. She likes it. "Don't you Kit? Tell him you like it." I get on her and I smell vomit and beer. Her mouth is all swollen. I think "I can't do this." But I do. Her eyes are closed and wet. Half way through she looks up at my face and right into my eyes. "I love you," she says. "I love you."

Cornelia
Mark V. Olsen

Scene: the Governor's mansion, Alabama

Dramatic
George Wallace: mercurial politician. 40s

> *When Cornelia Wallace suspects her husband of political collusion with the Klu Klux Klan, he makes the following defense of his unsavory policy.*

WALLACE: Cornelia, lemme tell you something. When someone like me goes for the brass ring, well nobody's just gonna give it to you. That what you think? That just ain't reality. You gotta roll up your sleeves and throw your punches. A jab or two below the belt when the referee ain't lookin— *(He shrugs, no big deal.)* Kennedy or Johnson or Nixon—? You think they just rode into town on *their* white horses? Think they never cut a corner? Sheeet. Sure, when I get out there speakin' to folks I have to fuss at the colored a little, but I don't mean any of it. People let off steam with me. They get mad—like this New York cab driver who says to me, "these niggers been robbin' me blind and I'm gonna vote for you." Well, he goes into that booth and—yennnnnhh! he yanks that lever and he gets to feelin' better. That's better than if he went out and got himself all frustrated and hit somebody over the head. And that ain't an excuse, and I ain't cryin' about it—it's just the way it is. It ain't worth havin' conniptions over. *(Beat.)* Cornelia—? *(Half beat.)* Come on, now— *(Half beat.)* Honey, it don't mean a thing.

Cornelia

Mark V. Olsen

Scene: the Governor's mansion, Alabama

Dramatic
George Wallace: mercurial politician. 40s

> *In a failed attempt to resuscitate his political career in the years following his attempted assassination, Wallace tries desperately to run on imagined past glory.*

WALLACE: *(Winking; slyly.)* I got me bruises this big—all black and blue—that's what ol' Cornelia's done to me.

[CORNELIA: *(Grinning, "shocked.")* Oh, Darlin', hush now—]

WALLACE: That's right—Pinching me to remind me to turn mah best side to the cameras— *(Grandly.)* Bet you never thought you'd be back to see this—ol' George Wallace back in the driver's seat, runnin in the primaries for president again—! *(He waits for the compliment that doesn't come.)* Yawl thought I was dying, thought I was through with politics. That I'd be a vegetable the rest of my life. You wouldn'ta bet I'd be back in Florida and be the front runner four years later, would you—? *(Beat; the charm's not working.)* Course you wouldn't. Forget what yawl been readin' in the newspapers, all that psychology mumbo-jumbo. It's true, I've had to concentrate on recovering, but Ah've never been in a period of depression. With twelve bullet holes in me I can't hardly run up the stairs and holler hurray, but that's not losing the ability to look up at the stars at night— *(Slides an arm around Cornelia.)* or admire my wife in the morning—

[CORNELIA: *(Tense but smiling her best.)* Mark these words— when next January 21st rolls around, you're lookin at the man who'll be the 38th president of the United States.]

WALLACE: *(Impersonating David Brinkley.)* "President Wallace invited reporters to the Oval Office today and told them to get out of town!" "President Wallace today called on Congressional Leaders to donate half their salaries to the Daughters of the Confederacy." "President and Mrs. Wallace flew to the summer White House in Mobile today." You just can't quite see it, can you? You just can't believe it will happen. *(Wallace beams, but the anecdotes fall flat to silence. The banners blow in the wind; bunting falls to the ground. He becomes desperate for a recognition that doesn't come. With increasing force, flailing.)* I won nine states in '68—I was born in a house with no indoor plumbin' and won eleven primaries in '72! I lived in a $5 a week room and washed clothes in the bathtub and lived on half-rotten potatoes—but I carried Boston!! *(Thundering, pleading for recognition.)* I carried Waltham and Brockton and Springfield and Newton and Quincy and Waymouth—AND I CARRIED BOSTON!!

Corpus Christie

Terrence McNally

Scene: a desert wilderness in Texas

Serio-Comic
Truck Driver: a man who knows his way through the wilderness.
40–60

> *Here, a weathered truck driver discusses the effects of driving across the desert with a hitchhiker.*

3RD TRUCK DRIVER: That's the desert for you. This is the scary part of the trip. Miles and miles of desert up ahead. Nothing but sand and heat. Not a place you want to break down. I did once. Left me a changed man. I had to hug myself at night to stay warm and make my own shade at high noon. You ever been alone like that? It can drive a person crazy. I thought I saw Anita Ekberg offering me a glass of ice cold milk. She was a Swedish actress before Your time. Famous for her tits. I told her I loved her and she just laughed, the way all mirages mock and deceive us, and let the cold milk run down her creamy breasts and vanished, only to appear again on the next horizon. We all have mirages we chase after. Mine was flesh. Wonder what yours'll be?

The Crustacean Waltz

R. Thompson Ritchie

Scene: an inn on an islet in the Chesapeake Bay, 1995

Dramatic
Jon Kinmartin: a freshman congressman, secretly gay, 47

> *When Jon and his lover decide to go public with their rela-*
> *tionship, they feel the only way to salvage Jon's political*
> *career is to keep a low profile for the remainder of his term.*
> *Unfortunately, this means that Jon can no longer sponsor a*
> *controversial bill regarding genetic testing, which he*
> *promised his late wife's sister he would do. When she angrily*
> *tells him that he owes it to the memory of his wife to spon-*
> *sor the legislation, Jon tells her exactly why he feels that he*
> *doesn't owe her anything.*

JON: Sweetheart, I don't owe Harriet anything—I sat by her bed
and held her hand for fourteen months—I was there for every
appointment, for every second opinion, for every x-ray and
exploratory procedure and high dose chemotherapy and plat-
inum treatment and gold treatment and…shit!…every fucking
torture they could dream up for her—I turned myself inside out
for your sister because I loved her and because she needed me
and because not once, not for one single minute that we were
married did she live for another person except me—And after she
died in that hospital room—while I was asleep in that chair next
to her bed, I did not sleep again for one solid year—no matter
what drugs I took or how much alcohol I poured down my
throat—not one night without nightmares, waking up in a panic,
sweating and terrified, living it all over again…Christ, Nay! Seven
years of therapy, and I'm just beginning to feel there might be a
life after your sister—So don't tell me I owe Harriet.
    [NAY: I need you now.]
JON: I'm sorry, Nay—I have to take care of myself for a while. Just
a little while.

Daddy's Heart

Nannette Stone

Scene: a living room, 1965

Serio-Comic
Uncle Ed: a retired railroad engineer and self-appointed family wiseman. 60s–70s

> *Here, Uncle Ed sips milkweed wine while watching the Tonight Show and discussing the future with his grandniece.*

UNCLE ED: Forget what your geometry teacher says. I tell you there is no such thing as a circle. You know God made everything round. The sun the moon. The seasons in a year. The rings that form when you drop a pebble in a pond. If a line goes on long enough it just meets itself. Anyone who thinks different just doesn't understand God's sense of infinity.

> *(There is the sound of applause and then of Johnny Carson laughing on the TV.)*

UNCLE ED: Just listen to that Johnny Carson laugh. You can tell a lot by the way a man laughs. Hear how open his heart is. Why that old JC could be anything he wants to be. Inventor…composer…Pope! Oh this? *(He takes a big swig out of the jar.)* Now don't worry my sweet. Milkweed wine just helps you see things more clearly. It doesn't make you a bit tipsy. Now that is what you wanted right my child? You wanted me to tell your future. Hmm. What you wanted? Well now that's just the point isn't it Sweet, almost anyone could tell the future if they were able to look at what is instead of what they want to see. Hmmm Well… *(He puts one hand over his eyes.)* You will have the opportunity to marry someone you love but you won't. You won't appreciate your mother until it is too late. Oh and…hmmm. Well Ronald Reagan will be president of the United States. All the elm trees are going to die. Oh and in 1999 there will be a huge earthquake and the

Mississippi river will disappear down a dark steamy hole some-where around St. Louis. Now stop giggling. Mark my words it is all true. And stop putting your faith in science and common sense. Think we are any smarter than those people who thought the world was flat? To know the truth of something you have to know how to go around in circles. The world turns, Mae. The world turns.

Dating Dummies

Elizabeth Ruiz

Setting: Santa Clara, Cuba

Serio-Comic
Cosmo: an alien with a good pick-up line. 20–30

> *Cosmo has traveled all the way to Cuba in search of an earth female with whom he can mate. Here, he does his best to impress a dubious young woman.*

COSMO: I ama your friend from outerespace. I hava been watching you. You are a special creature. Very imaginative in your head *(Points to his chest.)* and your heart *(Points to his head.)*. You hava natural understanding of de…big…big picture—even though you are a little escared to explore this.

[ESPERANZA: What are you doing here?]

COSMO: Well, it is kind of a long story, *but I will try to make it shorter.*

[ESPERANZA: What happened to your voice.]

COSMO: *Oh! That. I am an androgynous creature. In Trismegisdoro we are of both sexes. When we come to earth, we take on the sex that we need, to fulfill our missions.*

[ESPERANZA: Missions?]

COSMO: *Yes. Right now, I have no need to disguise myself, so when I am in my natural, relaxed state my voice changes from what you earthlings would identify as girl voice to a* boy voice *and back again.* Of course this happens only when we try to speak with words, in your earth languages. In Trismegisdoro we do not communicate with words. *Words for us are an archaic, although we believe, beautiful form of expression. We haven't much use for them…no more. Except when we put on our* twister espectaculos.

[ESPERANZA: Ehh?]

COSMO: Twister espectsculos. They're an ancient art form, very much like your "theater." They are the only art form we have left that employs the use of words. We call them twisters because they distort reality so much. However, it is a fascinating distortion, which although it causes much trouble, *it can be very exciting.* Things are not as exciting on Trismegisdoro as on earth. Too much harmony, I guess. But then, we haven't much use for excitement anymore. *(Flirtatiously.)* Not that we don't get excited, but it's different. We are a very old species. If now and then we need to get excited in the way that you earth creatures get excited, we go to the Twister Espectaculos *for a little distraction.*

[ESPERANZA: Why do you speak with an Italian accent?]
COSMO: Oh. I have only visited two earth locations, the first was Italy when Michelangelo was painting the Sistine Chapel *(With a wave of his hand he makes the Sistine Chapel appear to Esperanza and then disappear.)* and now here. The Italian seemed to have stuck, and at my age, three million three hundred and thirty three years, it's hard to lose your accent.

[ESPERANZA: So, if you are from a more advanced civilization, what are you doing here, in Santa Clara, Cuba?]
COSMO: Well, it's like dis. *(He motions for her to have a seat on a tree stump.)* I will try to explain with these words of yours. I keep de male voice, eh? Ah. *(He produces a demi tasse and a small saucer, hands it to Esperanza and pours espresso into the cup through his pinkie.)* The planet earth, is and has been a wonderful training ground for all of the entities of the universe.

[Esperanza takes a sip.]
COSMO: Good eh? It is a place that is both sad and beautiful, dull and fascinating, full of pleasure and pain to very big extremes. However, for a couple of thousand years, you have been stuck in a certain, how can I say era, dictated by the planets and constellations, and unfortunately, although it was to be an enormous period of growth, you are not progressing very well. Many things have gone really wrong. The two most obvious things are the destruction of all that is alive and the complete, undeniable *(Looks in his dictionary.)* ...animosity! between the male and the

female. How you men and women war with one another!!! Part of that is as it should be but it has gone too far. I see that forty or fifty years from now, two-thirds of the female populazione will be alone and without children. How will the species continue? It's very sad. The elders are looking at the possibility of jest letting you earth creatures destroy yourselves, but we're not sure yet. In the meantime, *(He puts his arm around her shoulders.)* we are coming down and mating with you, so that we can begin a new, more advanced, civilized and espiritual species.

(She stands up abruptly.)

COSMO: A species closer to us! Brand new, and yet full of the ancient wisdom of our sacred origins. But, I don't want to bore you, I jes wanted to know if you want to go for a ride in my hot wheels.

[ESPERANZA: Why?]

COSMO: We want to learn more about you, so that we can continue to improve our plan of action. At first we came into the dreams of your people. Then we appeared in visions, usually during times of despair. *(Relishing this.)* Not that I like to see you all suffer, but despair, believe me, it's the best way to progress when you are… *(Looks up word in his little book.)* in…in…inherently stupid. Now we are coming down and making de great love with your especies…but still there is much to learn. A person, of such purity of heart as you, Esperanza, you lovely, *(Looks at her flirtatiously.)* would be a very easy to study subject. Pleasant, efficient. We don't like taking people by force so we approach dose we feel may volunteer.

The Dead Boy

Andrew C. Ordover

Scene: here and now

Dramatic
The Dead Boy: a murdered child. 8–15

> *Here, the sad spirit of a murdered child speaks of the moment of his death.*

DEAD BOY: At the moment of my death
I saw my body dying
They held my head
And made me look,

My body over there
Not me
Larger than it looked
When I wore it

I saw my body dying
For one second still mine
For one second still me

It went rigid
And then soft
Folding in on itself
And falling to the ground

I opened my mouth to scream
To scream with no voice
To scream with no breath
I opened my mouth and died

They held my head
And made me watch
My body turn to garbage
This was my last sight on earth

Dog
Molly Louise Shepard

Scene: a bar in East Texas

Dramatic
Rick Jones: a man who can't forgive himself. 30s–40s

> *Rick has been haunted for years by the tragic suicide of a girl in his school. Here, he reveals why he feels responsible, in part, for her death.*

RICK: *(Pause.)* Well, look. This is the deal. I've been keepin' somethin' inside me all this time. It's just been botherin' me. I just gotta'… *(Pause.)*

That's when it all started. I couldn't even get the girl's attention. Ever. Man. She wouldn't even look at me. Do you know what that's like? To have someone not even acknowledge your friggin' presence? To be a complete zero? *(Pause.)*

See, it all started when Dog, I mean Dogavitch, I mean Patti started ninth grade. Remember? Everybody thought she was a new Senior. Kind of big, and voluptuous. Like Jane Mansfield. All the girls hated her at once. Thought she was a bitch. Said she was stuck up. She didn't talk to nobody. I wondered later if maybe she just couldn't. You know? Maybe she was just shy. That's all. Least that's what I think. *(Pause.)*

She sat right in front of me in Ms. Ebersole's English. Me and her, Geezler, Edmunds, Colton, Fredricks, all of us had most of our classes together. 'Cept electives. It was like that for years. Don't know if it was for alphabetic reasons, or intelligence. Who knows? So anyway, we have all these classes together. *(Pause.)*

When the teacher first called role, and she got to Dog. Well. You know, she calls out "Patti Dogavitch," and everybody laughs. Patti just says, "Here," quietly. We couldn't help it. You know? It was funny. And one thing led to another. Me and Geezler looked at one another, I think. I think it was me, that started barkin'. And then Geezler started barkin'. Then Edmunds and Colter, and Fredricks, and maybe even a couple of girls started in with it. Pretty soon we had stopped class. *(Whistles.)*

But Geezler man, he was the worst. Some person to be teasin' somebody about their last name, huh? He'd say, "Here, girl. Want it? Want it bad? Here pooch. Here rover. I got a dog biscuit. Want some chow, hound? Want it bad, yeah, you want it. You want it real bad. Here Lassie, come here, what is it, is it Frank? He hurt? Speak girl, speak!!! Ruf-ruf-ruf-ruf-ruf. Awroooo!!!" *(Howls and barks and salivates like a rabid dog for one minute.)*

And on and on like that. Yeah. I mean, we were just havin' a good time. *(Pause.)*

Seemed like Geezler took out every bit of meanness he had in his soul on Dog, I mean Dogavitch, I mean Patti. Anyway, it's weird. *(Pause.)*

So. Like, then things sort of…escalated. I was just tryin' to get her attention at first. See, she wouldn't look at me, she wouldn't talk to me. I hated the way she always knew all the answers in History class. Part of me wanted her to talk. But only to me. And to nobody else. *(Pause.)*

Oh, yeah. That was perfectly amazin'. Those huge breasts. Who could explain that? Huh? Big breast and a brain. Freak of nature. Hah-hah! *(Pause.)*

But the thing is, Ray. Is, I. Just wish. It'd never happened. Why couldn't she have gone to a different school. Or had a better name. Or been plain Jane. Or something. Or not so different. They say that wild dogs will attack a new member trying to join the pack. Just 'cause they're different. I watched on a nature special once. Will attack and destroy something different. Weaker. Makes me think we're not so very far from our more feral brothers, after all. It makes me think now…she was a little too sensitive. To like survive. Even maybe if she'd been able to take a joke, handled it different. Said anything. Why didn't she ever say, "Stop it?" Huh? Why didn't she, Ray? 'Cause I bet if she'd said

23

to stop, we would have. Before. Things got so out of hand. Everyone doing it. Calling her names. Other names, really bad things. "Dog" was bad enough though. I remember her walking into a pep rally, and the whole school barking at her. Who has to live through that? She. If she'd had a plain last name, like me. You know? She'd probably have been real popular. So pretty. *(Pause.)*

She sang "Scarborough Fair" in the talent show one year. She beat out the Ralph Gerling's Elvis imitation. He was a sure bet to win. If only 'cause he was the quarterback. Shoot, she had a pretty voice. Though. *(Pause.)*

I tried to congratulate her, but all she said was, "Thanks, Rick. Ruf, ruf." *(Pause.)*

I got pissed, and never really tried to be nice to her again. I was never mean to her the way the other kids were. To the degree they were. But. I never went out of my way, either.

So the thing is. I. Wish I hadn't started it. 'Cause maybe if I hadn't started it. She wouldn't have. Off'd herself. I was thinkin' that at the reunion. I was listening to "Leila," watching everybody dance. Fat Ruby Olston started rubbin' all up against me wantin' me to…dance. Whatever. 'Cause she heard Becky and me were separated. Breakin' up. The scene. It was just like when we were in High School. Disco mirror ball. The Hustle. Except everyone was really fat and bald and ugly. And it occurred to me. It hit me. If I hadn't started barkin', bein' the class clown. Trying to be funny…Patti Dogavitch blew her brains out because of what we did. I wish I'd never started it. Man. I wished to God I never started it. Why'd I have to be such a stupid, stupid kid. Huh? *(Beat.)*

So. But. The weird thing was. I mean, do you remember this? That she didn't have no funeral. Why was that. Was she an atheist or what? After being forever the underdog. I could sort of see why. I heard she was cremated, and her ashes sprinkled in the Gulf. Do you think that's true? Or just another rumor about her. Patti Dogavitch dust. One with the sea. *(Pause.)*

Sometimes when I think that I'm nothing, that I'm zero, that the world might not notice if I was gone or not, I think of Patti Dogavitch. Of the ripples she left behind. *(Pause.)*

I sort of missed her. Empty seat in front of me. Missed her at the reunion. I always did like lookin' at her. Her last name wasn't part of who she was anyway. It was just a name. *(Beat.)*

You think I'll ever be forgiven. Do ya'? *(Stands on chair, with gun in hand. Slowly raises gun in direction of face, hands shaking.)*

(Blackout. Sound of single shot, gunfire.)

The Dreamers

Christina Harley

Scene: Melody County, North Carolina. April 4, 1968: the day of the assassination of Reverend Martin Luther King

Dramatic
Otis: a bitter man crippled by polio. 35

> *Frustrated by his sister's faith in prayer to solve the family's problems, Otis here unleashes stored spleen.*

OTIS: *(Fed up.)* What you prayin' for Jesus to do, Lola? Huh? What's Jesus supposed to do? Well, answer me this. How long did yawl pray for my leg. Huh? How long? And what did Jesus do. *Nothin'.* Look at me. I ain't good for nothin' now. Can't go nowhere, can't do nothin'. King and his dreams. King and his dreams! Well, I ain't got no dreams no more. "I have a dream. I have a dream." What dream brother? And how was your dream supposed to help me? I used to have dreams. When I was seventeen I used to dream all the time. I dreamed I was gonna be the greatest runner there ever was. I was on my way, too. Gonna run faster than Jesse Owens! Compete in the Olympics. Surprise everybody whoever said I wasn't ever gonna be nothin'. Yeah, I was on my way. Wasn't I?

[LOLA: *(Softening.)* You were.]

OTIS: Daddy said I wasn't ever gonna be nothin'. Well, he was right. He said I was just a low down, dirty rotten no good sinner, chasin' the dreams of the world. Said God was gonna get me for that. *(To their father's portrait.)* Well look a here, daddy! You were right! How does it feel daddy! You were right! As always you were right.

The Dreamers

Christina Harley

Scene: Melody County, North Carolina. April 4, 1968: the day of the assassination of Reverend Martin Luther King

Dramatic
Al: a coal miner in love. 40s

> *Here, a very unusual coal miner reveals his love for Lola, a longtime friend.*

AL: *(Quoting Shakespeare.)* "But soft...what light through yonder window breaks. It is the East and Lola is the sun...etc. *(Al completes the Romeo monologue.)* On my sixteenth birthday, my mother gave me two huge books. One was a collection of Shakespeare's plays. The other was a huge black bible. My mother always said that God was the only white man we had on our side. According to her, the way to beat the white man at his own game was to learn to speak like him, while at the same time, pray to the white God to get the inside scoop. So there I was everyday after school. Memorizing my bible, then memorizing Shakespeare. Moma told me that all that memorizing would prove helpful to me someday. So far it hasn't. Who am I? I'm a forty-five-year-old colored man working in a dirty coal mine running down who begat whom to any and every able-bodied listener while trying to explain that Shakespeare really did write a whole play about a black man. That surprised them. Then they went back to work. That's who I am...What happens to us from the time we're six years old to the time we're forty? Not even forty, thirty, sometimes, even twenty. What happens? At six we see all the good in the world, feel all our potential, have the faith that nothing exists outside of love. And then...I don't know. I just know it's a shame that I can recite the titles of each and every Psalm without missing a beat, but my mouth won't form the words to tell Lola I love her…The sight of that woman…the smell of that woman…She makes me completely immobile. I feel like a seventeen year old…King talked about dreams…making dreams come true…I don't know. It all sounded good…I heard him talk about everything that could be available to us. Then…I look around and I see the little that *is* available to us. I just see the same old people doing the same old things. How can anything more be available than what I see?

Dutch Treat

Martha King De Silva

Scene: a restaurant

Comedic
Emmett: a guy who understands the bottom line of dating. 20s–30s

A six month anniversary celebration turns nasty when Emmett gets out his calculator.

(Emmett is seated at a table in a restaurant with his date.)
EMMETT: Shall we get the check? *(He looks to the waiter.)* When you're ready, we'll take the check. *(He reaches over to grab the hand of his date.)* Geez. Our six month anniversary, huh? It's hard to believe. Where does the time go, you know?

It's funny. *(He sips his drink.)* When you get to that point, it's not just dates anymore. *(He nods.)* Right. It's a relationship. *(He bites his lip.)* I mean I'm not seeing anybody else and you're not seeing anybody else. *(He sips his drink again.)* And, frankly, I start thinking about what I'm getting out of the 'relationship' versus what I'm putting into it. Well, I don't mean it exactly that way, of course. God, that sounds horrible. *(Pause.)* But lately, Barbara, well, I've been thinking. And what I've been thinking is that I'm putting much, much more into this 'relationship' than what I'm getting out of it. And, well, frankly, if we're going to go on with the relationship, and that's something I want, well, I think some things need to change. Oh, no honey. It's nothing that can't be fixed. I've just been mulling over things that I might change, if I could change them and.

Okay. Here's what I mean. *(He puts his briefcase on the table.)* I came across all these receipts the other day and it hit me. Hang on a sec and you'll see what I'm talking about. *(He pulls out a stack of papers.)* I put together a spreadsheet of our relationship. Now before you get all…just have a look.

Here's where I started from. Column A is a list of the dates that we've gone on and what they have cost. Let's start with October 3rd, our first date. I thoroughly enjoyed that by the way. We went to the movies and then out for coffee afterward. It was $7.50 apiece for the movie; $5.50 for your Kahlua and Coffee; $4.75 for my Nutty Irishman. I have the receipts here if you want to check. Okay. The total which I paid for on that date was $25.25. That's not including the gas and depreciation on my car. Okay. The total which you paid on that date was 0. All right. It's a first date. Kind of what I expected. And we had a nice time.

Now if you look closely, you'll see that Column A—my column—continues to be full of numbers throughout the relationship. The dinner at L'Auberge Chez Francois, the weekend at the beach, the sailing trip in Annapolis. In fact, when you consider the total it's quite astounding. I had no idea I had spent so much. $2,242. Wow. Over six months. That comes out to… *(He pulls out a calculator.)* over $373 per month. That's a lot of cash. All right.

Let's go to your column—Column B. $24 in column B for the night that you had me over for dinner. If I'm underestimating the dinner, I'm happy to be corrected on this point. But as I recall it was a meatloaf, some potatoes, and a bottle of wine. $24 is probably about right. $24 over six months. That means you spent, well, $4 a month on me since the relationship began.

[She begins to object.]

EMMETT: Now just wait a minute. Let's have a look at column C. I've put checks in Column C on the number of times that there was sex associated with the date. Okay. This is very important, I think. Let's go back to the first date. $25.25. Movies and coffee. No sex. That's fine. I didn't expect it, really. It was a first date.

[She gets angry.]

EMMETT: No, no, you're absolutely right. There was no discussion of sex at all. It was a kiss at your front door. Let's move down Column A a bit—my column—and see what happens. Date number two on October 11th, total for the date $47.61, no sex. Date number three on October 15th, total for the date $38.97, still no sex, what's this note I made, ah, some heavy petting, 3rd base. Ah-hah! Date number four. Dinner at Filomena's, $101.33. Sex. All right. But here's the point. I spent $213.16 before we even had sex once. And, well, I think that's, well, that's not insignificant to me.

Now let's compare Column C with Column A and I think you'll see what I'm getting at. With the exception of the meatloaf on December 2nd, Column A—my column—is completely full. But Column C is not so full.

[She begins to give examples.]

EMMETT: I know. We don't have to have sex everytime we have a date. On January 3rd you lost your job and were upset, and of course I didn't expect you to have sex. February 19th is another case. It was the weekend we visited your parents. We talked about it and that counts for something, but we didn't actually do it because you felt uncomfortable having sex in your parents' house. Now I think I could have found a way to sneak into your bedroom to have sex with you quietly without your parents ever knowing but I didn't. I respected your wishes. There are a number of occasions here, however, when it seems as though we could have had sex and we didn't and we didn't because *you* didn't want to.

What complicates this even more is Column D. Column D relates directly to Column C. And it's more or less my evaluation of, well, how good the sex was. Would you please sit down a minute and listen? Let's go back to date number four. Dinner at Filomena's. The dinner that I paid for that cost $101.33. A great dinner. And it was the first time we had sex. But, truth be told, the sex was not outstanding. And I think you'd agree with me on this. You had a little too much to drink, I think, and on a scale of one to five, with five being out of this world, it got a two. A sex score of two for a dinner costing $101.33 at Filomena's.

All right. So, here's the deal. I am perfectly happy for Column A—my column—to continue as before. And I'm perfectly happy as well for Column B—your column—to continue as before. If that's the case, however, we have to talk about substantive, meaningful changes to Column C. And we've got to take a long look at Column D. Lots of twos and threes in Column D and frankly, I'd like for that to change as well. I don't think it's too much to ask for a couple fours and maybe a five once in awhile.

Now I could get ridiculous with this thing and add another column—Column E. Opportunity costs for me. Women that I could be having sex with but am not because I'm dating you. But that would be absurd.

[She gets angry.]

EMMETT: I know that. And, if you would let me finish, please don't interrupt me Barbara, of course, what I also haven't included on this spreadsheet are the-uh, the intangibles. The non-quantifiables. The sort of psychic rewards to the relationship. And there are some. It's great not having to worry about what to do on a Friday night. You're a good listener. And when people ask me if I have a girlfriend, well, it's pretty terrific to say that, yes, I, Emmett Jones, have a girlfriend. But do those psychic rewards equal $2,242? I don't think so.

The point is not to point fingers at what's wrong with the relationship and who's responsible. Though I think the evidence shows, that you are probably more responsible than I. The point is.

[She interrupts.]

EMMETT: Sure we can talk about Column B, but actually, Barbara, I'm more concerned with Column—What do you mean your expenses? *(He indulges her.)* Like what? *(He listens.)* Your prescription for? Ortho-what? I don't know what that is.

[She shouts the answer.]

EMMETT: Oh, *that*. Oh. *(He is embarrassed; under his breath.)* I agree. I don't want to take any chances either. Better safe than. *(He speaks sotto voce.)* How often do you have to get that filled? And how much does it cost? *(He yells.)* FOR THOSE TINY PILLS?

[She says something else.]

EMMETT: $100 for waxing. Waxing? Oh, they were very smooth.

Yes, of course. It's just that. *(Meekly.)* You don't think you could have used a razor for that? Okay, okay. A $200 bill from Victoria's Secret? For that flimsy black thing? The one with the? No, I just meant…What else?

(The lights begin to fade.)

EMMETT: All right. $60. A French manicure. *(He sighs.)* $148. Cocktail dress at Ann Taylor. $37. In quarters. Washing your sheets.

(End of Play.)

The Dying Gaul

Craig Lucas

Scene: Los Angeles

Dramatic
Jeffrey: a film producer embarking upon an affair. 30–40

> *Married Jeffrey is attracted to Robert, a brilliant young screen writer. Here, Jeffrey takes a moment to reflect on his desire and how it impacts his life.*

JEFFREY: Sometimes when I'm holding him…the idea that this is a man, here, his heart beating through two skins, his…scent, his breath in the hollow of…his life in my arms. It's the same sometimes if I stop and I realize I make more money in one year than all of my ancestors did in all their lifetimes combined…the sense that truly there are no limits. And all the admonitions, the choruses of—ten thousand years of "Don't! No! You mustn't, don't eat tomatoes, they're poisonous! Don't be proud of your accomplishments, lie about what you want, who you are…Don't touch another man, god!" The miserable pile of accumulated human…deprivation…And all I do…all I ever do…is give people pictures of what they desire, *fantasies,* and—for eight dollars— and in return, if *the worst* I ever do is hold this man… unseen…here in this room…and love him…

The Engagement

Richard Vetere

Scene: Queens

Serio-Comic
Jeffrey: a world-weary divorce attorney. 30–40

> *Here, a guy who's seen it all when it comes to divorce offers
> the following cautionary tale.*

JEFFREY: Don't tell me! You think I'm overreacting? I'll give you something to overreact to—think about this: almost half of everybody you know who is married today, will wind up getting divorced! And when have you heard of a divorce that was amicable? I'll tell you what I think, I think people get married with stars in their eyes and they get divorced with guns in their hands! And when it's divorce they want that's when they come walking into my office with *hate* in their eyes! Hey, pal, I sit through these divorce cases! And it...amazes me! The brutality! The horror! People who held hands like children, people who swore to love each other forever, people who slept in the same bed together night after night, turn into vicious animals! I just finished a case yesterday where I represented this very sweet guy who was suing his wife for divorce after eight years of marriage. He paid me twenty thousand dollars and kept us in court for two years just to stop his wife from getting ownership of a broken-down hassock! When we won, he threw the hassock in the garbage!

[PAT: My God.]

JEFFREY: And they were childhood sweethearts!

The Engagement

Richard Vetere

Scene: Queens

Serio-Comic
Tom: a man on the verge of leaving his wife. 30–40

> *Ennui has claimed Tom's former passion for his wife. Here, cowardly Tom prepares a "Dear Jane" tape.*

TOM: *(Facing camera.)* Denise, I am taping this for you now while you're asleep in the bedroom because I am a coward…You know I am not as tough as people think I am. You are probably the only one who knows that. So that is why I am leaving this tape for you…I want you to move out tomorrow. I will get a room at a hotel until you are out…I can't let this messy relationship go on forever…I like my freedom! You are too much of a hassle! I can live without you! *(Tom shuts off the camera.)* Oh, what the hell… *(He puts the camera back on. To camera.)* This is the truth, Denise. Why I can't see or live with you anymore. *You got boring.* I mean, I come home and you're still sitting down in front of the TV. When we go out you say the same things all the time. You talk about the restaurant, your sister, your mother. You know the same people we knew when we met three years ago. You don't read any books. You don't like the movies. You don't care about my business. But that's not the way I remember you were when we first met. I remember when we talked at the party on Second Avenue that night, how exciting you looked. How interested you were in politics, sports and how you planned on going back to school. *I was really impressed. (Pause.)* What happened to you, Denise? Once you moved in all we did was complain to each other and fight about silly things. You even lost the certain light in your eyes. The light I saw there the night I first met you. *(Pause.)* Who took that away from you? Who? I'd really like to know who changed you. Who changed you from that exciting girl you were at the party? *(Pause.)* I'll tell you what I liked so much about you when we first met…it was that you were so *different* from me. You know I am a pretty dull guy. You know I don't like myself much. I don't like to read. I don't like the movies. I don't really like my business much. I was hoping you'd change *me* and not the other way around. Wow… *(Tom shuts off the camera. He finds a note Denise left him. Reading note.)* "Tom, wake me when you get home…no matter how late. I miss you. Love and kisses, forever and forever, Denise." Man, I can't live without you. *(Tom erases the tape and enters the bedroom. Lights out.)*

Erotic Scenes in a Cheap Motel Room

Michael Hemmingson

Scene: a cheap motel room

Dramatic
Gary: a man desperate to save his marriage. 30–40

> *Gary and his wife have agreed to meet in a cheap hotel in an effort to put a little zing back into their love life. Here, Gary waits in the room for his wife and ponders the state of their marriage.*

GARY: There must be a story in this. A story I'll write. The first sentence will be: "I got the room, like she said." The second sentence will be: "I waited an hour for my wife in that motel room." The third sentence will be: "She didn't show up." The fourth. I don't know. The story hasn't gotten that far. Lori suggested this last night. She said, "We need spark, we need pizazz, we need adventure and excitement." I was agreeable to any propositions. She suggested meeting in a seedy motel, she said she knew one that was perfect. I didn't ask her how she knew. I liked the idea, myself. I liked the idea of having her somewhere different, as I'm sure other men have had her; men I don't know about.

You see, yes, you see: I know about my wife. I know about her, say, extracurricular activities. I don't know much—I don't know who, when, or even why; I don't know how many there are. I just know. You're married to someone for ten years, you know. I was playing drums in this band when I first met Lori. (I don't play the drums anymore.) We were playing this one club a lot and Lori was a waitress there and doing her internship and we started to date. On the third date, we fucked in my studio apartment and it was great. I knew one day I would love her; I knew one day I would marry her. When I asked her, finally, a year or so later, if she wanted to get married, she said, "Yes, I do." I wanted to write short stories and novels instead of pounding on drums, and so I did, and Lori started to work in the medical profession, working as a radiologist, while I wrote my stories. Now I'm writing this story. "He thought he saw a cockroach run across the floor," another sentence will say, "but it must have been his imagination." "Why was he here," the story will go on, "when by all rights he should have left his wife by now." But I love her too much; I love her so much that I can forgive what she has done, whatever it is she has done, and in some way I suppose I don't blame her. Our marriage was falling apart, and I suppose it still is. But we can pick up the pieces. I have faith we can heal and go on. Maybe things just got too cozy. A little too boring. "We need excitement in our lives, Gary," she said, his wife said, he recalled his wife saying one night not too long ago, "remember when we were young and everything was exciting?" "We were poor," he replied, "never knowing what was going to happen to us the next day." "That's just it," she said, "we know what's going to happen tomorrow, we know that tomorrow will be just like any other day in our life, and that's what's killing me." She said "killing me," not "killing us." Doesn't she know what's killing me?

Evil Legacy

Kathrine Bates and Ted Lange

Scene: 15th century Rome

Dramatic
Cesare Borgia: powerful member of the infamous Borgia clan.
40s

> *Here, the scheming Cesare pays a visit to his sister, Lucrezia.
> He informs her of the family's recent attempts to bring the
> empire under Borgia control and warns her of the impending
> and untimely demise of her husband, Giovanni Sforza.*

CESARE: He is a fool, Lucrezia. A silly pompous fool. He thinks like
a lover. He is not a Pope, he is a school boy enthralled with a
young girl. When Giulia was captured...you haven't heard?
Where have you been keeping yourself, Lucrezia, in a convent?
Wake up to the business of the Vatican! You must know that
King Charles has an army just outside of Rome? Good. You are
not lost to the name of Borgia yet! Charles is making allies as he
marches toward us. He wants to reclaim the Vatican for God. Can
you imagine? That ugly little French dwarf, Charles of Valois. I
know prostitutes that would return his money and couple with a
goat before they would lie with the likes of that French pig!

King Charles! Ha! The Medici's, The Colonnas...and now the
Sforzas have all become allies. The Sforza family. The Sforza family! Yes, Your precious little Giovanni's clan. But our father's
thoughts are not focused on such things...oh, no. Dealing with
traitors is nothing compared to consoling the lovely Miss Farnese.
Curse these robes! If I had not been forced into the church I
would be at the head of the armies right now, dear sister, not that
inept fool of a brother. Juan, Bah! One day I will open Father's
eyes! I tell you, if it were me, that French pig would be tossed
back into the sea on the point of my sword...

Don't worry about your precious Giulia, my love. She is quite well. The irony of it! Father sends her off to Vitebo to keep her safe from the French, but on the way she is captured…by whom? The French! *(He laughs.)*

A patrol, just outside of Rome. Oh, she's all right. They didn't harm her. She probably gave herself to some French Lieutenant.

Then Charles turns around and offers her for ransom! Three thousand Ducants! Yes, Father paid it. Yes, yes, yes. He paid it! What is that old man thinking? Giulia is not an imbecile. She would have survived. Giulia Farnese is a beautiful woman. She is smart and likely very masterful between the sheets. Believe me, she would have survived. Now we have a problem. Now the French know his weakness. They were fools to let her go.

Which brings me to your weakness. Yes, you have a weakness. Giovanni Sforza! I know that he is your husband, but he is also part of the Sforza family. These are perilous times, Lucrezia. Ludovico Sforza is this night supping with Charles of Valois. They are blood, Lucrezia, and blood takes care of its own. But I have a plan…No, not a ransom. Clear your thinking, little girl. The Papal throne is in jeopardy. We must send a message to that ugly French dwarf. After all, we Borgias speak for God, do we not?

I want you and Giovanni to sup at my table tomorrow night. We will have all his favorite foods and I will make sure the wine is red and hearty. Oh, I hear he has a sweet tooth…? Good, we will save that for dessert. Plenty of Marzipan. We will laugh and sing and tell stories and I will see what side of the fence this Sforza sits on. So you will make sure he comes to my table?…Good. You know that I love you? You are my sweetest angel. Am I still first in your heart?…That's my girl. Come at dusk, Lucrezia. *(He crosses to the door.)* I look forward to an entertaining evening. *(He stops at the door.)* Oh, Lucrezia, my darling, after we sup. Don't eat the desert. The Marzipan. Don't eat it. Let's just say…it won't agree with your stomach. The taste of something sweet can mask the true nature of many a demon. Ha, ha, ha, ha, ha, ha, ha, ha, ha, ha!

The Face of God

Justin Warner

Scene: Heaven

Serio-Comic
Brad: a harried young angel filling in for God. 20–30

> *God, it seems, has taken a leave of absence leaving Brad in charge of his many duties. Here, overworked Brad unloads on a new arrival to the celestial kingdom.*

BRAD: Yes! Acting God! That's my title, okay? I'm performing the duties of the Almighty with His full authority until that time that He returns!

[GRENDEL: Which is when exactly?]

BRAD: I don't know! The bastard just walked out! I've been stuck here taking care of his crap for sixteen years! And there's no vacation, Mr. Grendel. No golf weekends. Not even a bathroom break. If you leave your heavenly post for even a second your soul gets destroyed! That's policy.

[GRENDEL: *(Interested.)* You don't say.]

BRAD: Oh, you don't know the half of it, pal. We've got poultry plant working conditions up here. Sure, we all take these jobs because we need the redemption, but let me tell you, Mr. Don't Take My Name in Vain rides that for all it's worth! I mean, even before he took off, he never really *did* anything. Just sat around, passed judgment, and read The Economist. And one day, I'm in here doing some filing, and the G-man says to me, "Brad, I'm going for coffee—could you mind the desk while I'm gone?" I said sure. That was the last I ever saw him! "I'm going for coffee." What the hell was that? I mean, he could just *zap,* make the coffee right there, right? How could I let him screw me over like that? If I ever see him again, I swear I'll kick his lazy omnipotent ass from here to Cleveland!

The Fathering

Jussi Wahlgren

Scene: an apartment in Germany

Dramatic
Thomas: a concert pianist; a stubborn genius. 20s

> *Lonely Thomas has sent for a piano tuner, even though his piano doesn't need tuning. The tuner turns out to be a drinking man, and Thomas here lectures on the virtue of hard work.*

THOMAS: Well, drink up old man. Heart pumps blood to the brains. That's what it does. It has a function in the human body. Unlike some of us in the human society. There's nothing irrelevant in the human body, nothing, er, how should I put it…

[PETR: There is a voice in your heart. I believe so, honestly. It tells you how you should live your life. It's very powerful if you let it come out. So to speak.]

THOMAS: Nonsense. You're just being bitter, because you're a caretaker and not the owner of the house, what ever it is, where you're working at. Am I right? And instead of being just a piano tuner you'd like to be a piano virtuoso, wouldn't you? Is that what your heart's voice tells you, eh? Well, sir, I can tell you that only a few of the millions of talented artists make it big. And that's because only a few of them work hard enough. It's very simple really. It takes creativity, which we all have. You painted pictures when you were a kid. We all did. And then it takes talent. Some of us have that. It's a God's gift, so to speak. But most talent go to waste. And only a fraction of all talented people make it. And why? Because they work hard, hard and hard. There's no other way. And drinking isn't helping a bit, believe me, sir. *(Takes the brandy bottle away.)*

[PETR: I'm not finished yet, I mean *(Points to the piano.)* with
the, the…Cheers. *(Drinks his drink and plays a few bars.)*]
THOMAS: The heart pumps blood to the brains. That's what it does.

Freak

John Leguizamo and David Bar Katz

Scene: here and now

Comedic
John Leguizamo: a performer remembering his youth. 20s–30s

> *Here, Leguizamo recounts an ill-fated attempt to pick-up an
> Irish-American colleen in a bar in Queens.*

JOHN: So I was an angry, disillusioned kid. And then we up-graded
to a poor all-Irish neighborhood in Sunnyside, Queens, where we
were the first Latin family, so we were like pioneers. Manifest des-
tiny in reverse. And I see this real hot Irish chick. You know the
type—red-headed, freckled, drunk, lapsed Catholic whore, ready
to be inseminated by a wily Latin stud. Okay, I'm bitter—they
never liked me. So I'm having some green beer, and since everybody's Irish on St. Patrick's Day I figured I'll try out my gift and
riverdance over to her, and I talk to her in the thickest Irish accent
I can manage.

"Toy, hello, lassie, how's the Emerald Isle? You ever fuck a
leprechaun? Erin go bragh and begorrah. Why are you looking at
me like that? Is my shillelagh hanging out? Are my shenanigans
banging about out?"

She took a long draw on her cigarette and said, "You don't
look Irish to me."

"Oh, but I am, black Irish." I lifted my beer. "I'm parched
above, lassie. Are you moist below?"

Okay, so I didn't say that. I said how much I respect Irish culture and what contributions they've made: U2, whiskey, cops,
and, of course, Scotty. "Captain, the dilithium crystals are breaking up, the engine she's gonna blow. The heath the moor you
know you got to go see *Trainspotting, Braveheart.* You sit

45

through the whole movie and you can't understand a word even if you see it forty times."

"What kind of fucking moron are you?" she asked.

"Scotty's Scottish, asshole. Everybody knows that. Brian, Sean, Blarney, this Spanish guy is bothering me."

Then ten or fifteen of her hooligan brothers circled me, proof that the rhythm method doesn't work in the Irish community. We Latin people, we have rhythm, but we save it for dancing.

"Are you trying to get with our sister, you dirty Puerto Rican?" asked the biggest Irish brother.

"Well, your mother was booked, now wasn't she?" I remarked.

"I'll wipe up the street with ya, you little wetback!" He took a threatening step in my direction.

"But where, laddie? Where's the lad with the moist back?" I cried out, looking all around the bar. "I'll give him a taste of me fisticuffs. Where's the little fucker? I'll find the little fucker and get him for you."

"You! You're the lying little spic!" He wasn't fooled.

I was outnumbered, but I didn't care. I did what any proud Latin kid raised in the ghetto would do in that situation, and I make no apologies. I—acted like a retard. "I didn't touch the pretty lady, no I didn't. I gotta pee. Hold it for me. Why won't you hold it for me? It burns. Come on, blow on it. Why won't you blow on it?"

Full Moon, Saturday Night

Amy Beth Arkawy

Scene: here and now

Serio-Comic
Famous Guy: a young man obsessed with celebrity and death.
19–20s

> *This lonely young man has phoned a crisis hotline in search
> of a sympathetic ear. Here, he complains to the phone vol-
> unteer about his lack of experience with women.*

FAMOUS GUY: Who I am? *(Pause, starts to cry.)* Who I am is someone who can't…who never…You know when I was eight I was
in love with this girl only she wasn't a girl, she was this friend of
my mother's only she wasn't anything like my mother or anybody
else's mother. Her name was Madeline Ventura and she looked
like Audrey Hepburn but she owned her own boutique. I remember going in there with my mother she had clothes and bath oils
and it always smelled so sweet…lilac, I think. Or rosewater. Then
she got married—for the third time, I think—to some business
honcho. And I went to the wedding and Madeline Ventura
danced with me and while we were dancing, this goddess, this
boyhood fantasy just out and out lied to me. She looked into my
eyes and said, "Just wait you'll break some hearts in your day."
(Raises voice.) Well, I'm still waiting! But what did she know? She
was just as messed up as every other suburban bimbo brained
bitch. I just made her up in my mind. Anyway, her husband, the
tycoon, got snagged by the SEC and did time in Danbury with
Reverend Moon and Leona Helmsley. I think she divorced him and
went on to number four or five *(Laughs.)* Some fantasy girl!
(Pause.) Oh screw it! Most famous people were geekazoids and
nerds before they were famous. So it's like some perverse reward.
Suffer alone until you're rich and famous and then have more
people to fuck than you know what to do with.

The Gift

Simon Fill

Scene: here and now

Dramatic
John: a suicidal young man. 14–16

> *John has been hanging out with Jones, a girl from school, all*
> *afternoon. They have spent their time talking about life and*
> *its many disappointments. Here, depressed John relates a*
> *story about a kid named "Edward" who is, in reality, John.*

JOHN: He got messed up…He found a diary. *(Pause.)* Edward. I
used to hang at his apartment a lot. In Chelsea—I could board
there from Delbert's. Like, it was a fucked up situation. So. It's in
some books his mom asks him to toss. Like, she owned a used
bookstore when he was born—and kept a lot of the shit after it
closed. Sometimes people'd leave their private stuff in what they
sold her. So. I open this old diary—and the first thing I read is,
"January 12th. Boiled an egg for breakfast." Like, it's the whole
entry for January 12th. It's, like, hilarious. We crack up. Then,
"January 18th. A catastrophe of onions." A catastrophe of
onions? I mean, please. What does that mean? We're, like, totally
losing it. Then, "January 21st. I could never love this boy. I wish
it'd never been born." We're, like, "Not only is this writer unbal-
anced, he or she's an asshole, too." He's laughing, I'm laughing.
Then he's, like, looking to see who wrote this, if there's a name
inside. *(Pause.)* His mom wrote it when he was four years old.
(Silence.)

[JONES: Like, time to give the babysitter some credit, eh?]
JOHN: It explained why his mother'd always been cold to him,
though he didn't really know why. After that, he didn't want to
hang out with me so much. It's, like, he associated me with something he never wanted to know. But we did have coffee once. It

was hilarious. I thought, "We're about to drink coffee, like grown-ups." Then I was like, "Wow. Coffee tastes like shit. What is up with older people?" He told me he was trying to see his father, his parents split when he was two. You see, his father'd stopped seeing him when he was, like, eleven. Like, the mother said the dad was busy, and it sort of just trickled out. I thought, "This is tragic, I should pay for the coffees." So. It's four years since he's seen his father, and he's trying to hang in his father's neighborhood. One day, he walks into someone. He looks up. It's his father. He thinks, "This is great." Then his father looks worried and goes, "Are you lost?" *(Pause.)* He didn't even know who Edward was.

Give Me Shelter

Wendy Weiner

Scene: NYC

Serio-Comic
Bull: a bullish Realtor. 30s

> *Diana is searching for an apartment in Manhattan. Here she*
> *comes face to face with the enemy: the Realtor.*

BULL: Hello, Diana, and welcome to Crowman Realty where we've got something to crow about. Badabing, badabang. I'm Bull. *(Vigorous handshake.)* And yes, Bull is my Christian name, not a nickname, nothing to do with my impeccable reputation as the only honest realtor in our fine jewel of a city.

Now, what has brought you to our office today? Mm-hmm Mm-hmm. The ad for the $600 studio in the West Village. Beautiful apartment, all right? Sun drenched, eat-in kitchen, working fireplace, not available. It means, it's taken. Apartments like that—they're gone yesterday. It's like puttin' a steak down in front of a group of hungry orphans. Before I can even put it on the barbecue, it's gone. Now, what I *do* have is a gorgeous studio a bit further west, only $1200.

Mm-hmm All right, all right, you need a lower price range. Have you thought about Brooklyn? No, no, you want to keep your search to Manhattan, let's see what we got. Ah! Here. If you like the West Village, you might be interested in Yorkville. Hmm? Well, no, the neighborhoods are quite different, but they *are* both in Manhattan and that's what you're looking for, right? Now, in Yorkville, I got what we call a "half-studio" for only $1150.

Look, I am sensing some attitude here. Did you read the *New York Times* magazine last May? I said—did you read the *New York Times* magazine last May? *(Holds up a magazine with the*

words *"Why it's So Hard to Rent an Apartment"* on the cover.)
Read it! Then maybe you'll have some idea what we're up
against.

(Suddenly beats his chest and gives out a long Tarzan yell.)
I'm a warrior, OK? That's how I see myself. An urban warrior in
the most ferocious jungle of a market that exists, has existed, and
God willing, ever *will* exist. And I need to know that you're a warrior too. I can not have a client who's gonna drop dead halfway
through—ooh, it's hot! ooh, the mosquitoes! ooh, I'm getting
blisters—is that an anaconda? Aaahhh! And then, I have to haul
your dead-weight carcass out of the jungle. Dead weight is heavy,
my friend…Are you a warrior? Louder! Are you a warrior? *(Beats
chest and yells again.)*

(Instantly business-like.) All right, how much is your annual
salary? You are joking with me, right? My nephew, who is seven
years old, earns more than that in allowance. That, I can tell you
right now, is gonna be a problem. See, you should be making ten
times the amount of your yearly rent. That's the kind of figures
I'm looking for.

All right, no salary to speak of. How about your credit? Your
credit? Do you have outstanding bills that you haven't gotten
around to paying? Are there people looking for you who might
want to outfit you with some concrete boots government-style?
All right And who will be serving as your guarantor in the tri-state
area? No one? No one at all? A cousin, an aunt, an ex-boyfriend,
someone your grandma knew from her heyday in the forties?

You, my friend, are out of luck. Badabing, badabang. I'll be
straight with you. I'm the best there is. Studios, one bedrooms,
two bedrooms, I got everything from the charming artists garret
on the Bowery to the Central Park penthouse with wraparound
views. But with these stats, there's not a damn thing I can do for
you. Not one damn thing. *(Pause. He looks at Diana uncomfort-
ably, then takes some Kleenex from a pocket and holds it out to
her.)* Tissue? *(Slaps hands together, checks watch. Standing up.)*
OK, kid. I got a 3:30

Give Me Shelter

Wendy Weiner

Scene: NYC

Serio-Comic
Ned: an affable slacker dude, 20s

> *Here, chatty Ned gives the grand tour of his Hell's Kitchen apartment to a possible future tenant.*

NED: Hey… come on in. I'm Ned…So, you're a "friend" of Tapio's? Oh, Jewel. Yeah. She's a great lady. Well, let me give you the grand tour. *(Points to right near the bed.)* This is the bedroom. This hot pot is the kitchen. And this *(Pointing again to right near the bed.)* is the living room.

Yeah, I measured it when I first moved in. It's roughly six feet by nine feet by seven feet. And, if you put a loft bed in, that would like double the space. Oh, the bathroom is in the hallway, right down there. You share it with the family on the other side of the hall. They are very nice people. Every one of 'em. Um, I don't know, there's…six of them, no, seven with the new baby. She was born right here in the building. *(Smiles thinking of her.)* Baby Sally. Oh, and the terrace— *(Lifts up window bars with difficulty, leans out window.)*

I covered this strip of tar with Astroturf and it's really killer. I hung out here all last summer and, as you can see, you have an excellent view of the alley. The rats are awesome. They're more like people than people think—there's families and gangs and sex stuff. If you don't have a TV, you can definitely kill hours that way.

Oh no, I'm not leaving cause of the apartment. It's been real great. Having your own casa in Manhattan is practically unheard of. No, I'm leaving for *(With mystery.)* "personal reasons." *(Long pause.)* Well, since you ask, last Thursday, I had a moment of clarity. NoZone, our band, was playing at Mercury Lounge, and we always end our sets with this song Tap wrote called "Age of Rage." So I'm playin' the rhythm. *(Starts beating out the rhythm with his foot.)* It's a real constant, driving beat, you know. Like when you're angry. And your heart's slamming against your chest. There's all this blood flowin' through you. You're starting to shake. You can't see. *(Stops beat.)* I don't know why, it was really gettin' to me. So after the set, I took off and walked out onto Houston Street, but the beat was still there. *(Starts beating out rhythm again.)* People pushin'. Horns honkin'. Subway rushing underground…all to that same beat. *(Stops beat.)* It's not a wonder people kill each other here, it's a wonder most of us are still alive.

Oh, the place? It's yours, if you want it.

The Golden Gate Bridge

Ludmilla Bollow

Scene: a roadside curb

Dramatic
Martin: a former astronaut who has deteriorated in both mind and body. 50–70

> *Near the end of a tasking cross-country journey, Martin has been reduced to being pulled along in a coaster wagon. When a group of children attack with taunts and sticks, Martin explodes with rage and frustration.*

MARTIN: What do you bastard kids know about astronauts!
[They retreat a few paces.]
MARTIN: Just because you saw a picture of one in your school books, you think you'll know one when you see one!
[They move in taunting, "Nah, nah, nah nah nah."]
MARTIN: You know so much! Just because you read it in a book! You don't know anything! About life—suffering. You don't learn those things from a book.
[They skip in a circle about him, still taunting. Martin rotates to address them. Shouting louder.]
MARTIN: Empty pages of inked up paper, that's all they are. Flat, lifeless pictures. They can't show you what's inside a person. How he thinks, feels! They tell you to get good grades. Rise to the top of your class. Then, presto, whamo, you're all prepared for life!
[They stop taunting and stand as if hypnotized.]
MARTIN: And if you're really top grade—you can even go to the moon! Yeah, that big wonderful gold medal in the sky. *(Slowing down.)* Only, once you get there, it's nothing but a pile of cold ugly rock. Powdery gray dust. Why the hell don't they teach you to look inside yourselves at those damn schools. Why are they always projecting you into some far distant future! *(A scream*

from within.) You don't exist out there! You exist within yourself. I can barely see…Hardly walk…But, I can still feel…Only nobody taught me what to do with these feelings. *(Breaking down.)* They taught me to read—with these eyes. Write—with these hands. But never what to do with these tears. Or how to get in touch with my soul! I've been cheated! So have you. *(Complete breakdown.)* And nobody's stopping them! Nobody's out there stopping them!

Horrible Child

Lawrence Krauser

Scene: here and now

Dramatic
Terrible: a killer. 20–40

> *Horrible Child's parents have engaged the grim services of Terrible, an assassin. When asked how he came to deal in death, Terrible makes the following reply.*

TERRIBLE: I used to kill bugs as a hobby.
The first beetle I squashed
broke like caviar in my palm.
There was always some kind of
unexpected beauty. A color, a
form, the twitchy hello of a
nerve that refused to succumb.
Once, in this way, a grass-
hopper I had choked to death
left a remnant of its life in a
single antennae, which was so
like a finger beckoning that I
took it for a sign. I came to
believe that Death was choosing
me. I moved on to more complex
forms of life, becoming
something of a local legend,
and when the time came to
settle on a career, there was
no doubt. I went into people,
for this was the most lucrative
market, and quickly proved to
be more accomplished and subtle

in technique than many of my peers who'd spent years in formal training.

Impossible Marriage

Beth Henley

Scene: a country estate outside of Savannah

Serio-Comic
Reverend: a man of the cloth who has gone astray. 20s–50s

> *The Reverend has been having an affair with Floral, who is married and pregnant. Here, the foolish man dramatically announces his intention to leave the church and the community for having wronged a parishioner.*

REVEREND: Floral, I'm so very grateful to have come upon you. I have some information to impart. Nothing noteworthy. In fact, a matter of no importance to anyone. I have come to the conclusion this evening that I must leave the church. It is not much, but it is all I have to sacrifice for my hypocrisy. I'm not a talented or impressive man. All I had to give the world was a few good deeds. I took the woman with no legs an Easter bonnet; I taught the blind child to sing; I allowed mosquitoes to suck my blood with impunity. All of this motivated by a desperate wish to have some value. And yet I betrayed it all. *(He looks away from her.)* The meaning of my life and the woman I esteem above all others. I beg her forgiveness. I do not expect it. In fact, I firmly believe forgiveness must never be granted. But I do crawl at your feet on my hands and knees now and always, and forever.

Killer Joe

Tracy Letts

Scene: a trailer home on the outskirts of Dallas, Texas

Dramatic
Chris Smith: a small-time hood and sometime dreamer. 20s

> *Chris has conspired with his father to have his mother killed
> for the insurance money. When the hired killer demands sex-
> ual favors from Chris's sister as partial payment for his deed,
> Chris gets cold feet. Here, Chris tells the killer of his one-time
> dream of being a farmer.*

CHRIS: I tried startin' a farm once. That seemed like the kind of life
I want. Workin' for myself, outside a lot, make my own hours, live
in the country, smoke dope, watch t.v. That's all I really want.

So I started a rabbit farm. I built the whole thing, by myself.
I was livin' with a coupla guys out near Mesquite, but they didn't
help me; I built it, with my own two hands. Lumber, chicken wire,
water bottles, pellets. Rabbits. I loved those little bastards. They
smell like shit, and they fuck all the time, but they're awful easy-
goin' animals.

I left for a coupla weeks, cause of this girl down in Corpus,
and when I got back, a rat, or a skunk, or somethin' had got in
the pen, and it was rabid. Awful hot out, too.

They just tore each other apart. Their eyes were rollin', and
foamin' at the mouth, and…and screamin'. Did you know rabbits
can scream? They sound just like little girls.

It was disturbing.

I started sellin' dope for a living. I knew more about it.

The Last Plea

Mark Bellusci

Scene: a court room

Dramatic
Tony: a desperate man at the end of his emotional rope. 40s.

> *When he is brought up on charges for stalking his estranged
> wife, Tony makes the following plea to the judge.*

TONY: Your Honor, I know you heard all the testimony and everything. And I know I've done some wrong here, there's no doubt
about it. But, you know, before you go and, uh, think it all
through, I just want to try and explain my side of the story—no,
I know my lawyer did that—and he did a damned—sorry, your
honor—a darned good job of it. But—and no offense to your
court or anything—it was all kind of legalese stuff. I just want to
explain it the way it really happened. You know, in plain English.
(Beat.) No no no, it won't take more than a minute or two. *(Beat.)*
Okay, so where do I—I don't know, I guess we started having
troubles a couple a years ago. Right after we had the kid, but
before we— *(Beat.)*

Okay, Your Honor. I was just setting up why what happened,
but—okay, so we're having troubles after the kid. Nothing big at
first, regular arguments like all my buddies have with their wives.
But for some reason, ours just got worse. Got so bad I didn't
wanna come home a lot of nights—and sometimes I didn't. I
mean, with the nagging and the kid crying and me trying to just
get a little peace after a hard day's work—you're a guy, your
Honor, you know. *(Beat.)*

Well, then you're the lucky one, Your Honor, cause most guys
I know, they know what I'm talking about 'cause they've been
there. But anyway, it keeps getting worse and worse—the yelling
and the screaming and everything. And I'm cutting outta there

more and more—just to avoid getting in fights with her. Well, one day, I come home after staying out all night, and she's got this look like a psycho killer. She's quiet at first, but then she starts hitting me—hitting me! Me, who never touched her in her life, she is hitting. And she's not stopping! She's whacking me! So after a while—and I'm a patient guy, I took some shots, my wife, you've seen her, she's built like a middle linebacker—after a while I gotta defend myself. *(Beat.)*

No your Honor, I never hit her. No sir! I just kept my hands up and tried to hold her off. I mean, if you saw us after the battle, I'm the one with the black eyes and shi—and stuff. She just had a couple a bruises on her arms where I held her. *(Beat.)*

That's exactly what I'm leading up to, your Honor. So after this little battle royale, after she beats the shi—the heck—outta me, she says *she's* moving out. You believe it? I get whacked around and *she* can't take it no more. So that's what she does—she ups and leaves, with the kid. Well Your Honor, I gotta be honest with ya, at first I felt great. I mean, really great. All the pressure off. No kid yelling and screaming, no woman nagging at me. It was like the old single days. But see, here's where it gets fuh—messed—up. See, as happy as I was when she left, I started getting miserable again. Like, all of a sudden, the house was too quiet. Actually missed the kid screaming—I even missed Julia's nagging. I mean, Your Honor, first she makes my life miserable by being home, then she makes my life even more miserable by *not* being home. I mean, we're supposed to be married, we're supposed to work through all that shi—stuff, right? And that's what I went over her house to tell her. *(Beat.)*

Yeah, I'm almost there, your Honor. Just another minute. So anyway, I go to her mother's house, tell her I'm sorry for our troubles and that she could come home. And you know what? She says she ain't coming home. Says I'm not ready for her to come home. Me? The one who got beat up? I'm not ready? So, naturally, I get a little pissed. Who wouldn't? I tell her I'm her husband and she's got to come home. So she boots me. Boots me! Her husband! Threw me out on my as—butt. And every time I come over after that, she don't even answer the door. But see, I'm not about to give up on our marriage that easy. I figure, If I could just talk to her—reason with her a little bit—she'll see the mistake she's making. So what I would do is just drive over and wait for her to come out. You know, just so I could talk to— *(Beat.)*

Yeah, your Honor, I know. But, see, I still can't figure out how that could be stalking if all I want to do is talk to her— *(Beat.)*

You're right, that's a done deal. We plead on that—but still— okay, never mind. So anyway, what happened after, that's what this whole thing is about anyway, and that's what I wanted to talk about. It was about a month ago. I was out earlier that night, at this club, La Mouche—hey, she's living the good life at her mothers, I might as well have a little fun too. So I'm talking to some young girl. She wants to dance, I dance with her. She wants to drink, I buy her drinks. She wants to giggle with her little girl friends about me being older, I just put on a dumb smile and deal with it. Next thing I know, we're in her car, grabbing and mauling, grabbing and mauling, and I'm into it—I mean, your Honor, I *am* a man with needs and everything. So I'm into it with this young girl whose name I don't even know, just like the old single days, you know? Then, outta the blue, I start thinking about Julia. Julia! Even when she's not there, she's there. Pissing me off, interfering where she's got no right to interfere. And me? I'm losing it with this hot, drunk twenty-one year old. So that's it, I decide. I tell this girl I'm not into it, she's too stoned to care, and I leave. So…I decide I can't enjoy fuh—messing—around, getting drunk, stoned anymore; might as well live with her. *(Beat.)*

No, it's not exactly a romantic way to put it, but that's the way I felt. And I wanted her to know, right then and there. So, I drive to her mother's house. Now I admit, it was late. But all I figured on doing was staying in the car, right in front of her house, be there as soon as she comes out in the morning for work. But then I get to thinking, it's hot and miserable in my goddamned car, why the hell do I have to sleep like a dog when she's in a comfortable bed. So I rang the bell. Told her I needed to speak to her. And you know what? She never even opened the door! Told me I'd better leave or she was calling the cops. And she did! She called the fuh—the frigging cops on her husband! *(He sighs.)* Well, I was gonna sit there in my car, let them take me in, you know? But, then I'm thinking, frickin' cops, why should their life be so easy when mine's a mess? They wanna get in the middle of my marriage, I'll make 'em work for their paycheck, those fat, lazy Irish bastards— *(Beat.)*

Sorry, your Honor. I didn't know you were part Irish. So—and I now know this was wrong, your Honor—I tear ass outta there. And the cops, they take off right after me. Next thing I know, I'm in a high-speed chase, just like the movies! Well, we're going pretty good, sixty on the side roads. Let me tell you, those guys stayed right with me. So there I am, going through the side streets, you know? But now there are more and more cops on my ass, so I figure, before they cut me off completely, I'll get on the highway, really open it up. So I get on the Belt, figuring if I could make it over the Verazano bridge and through Staten Island, I'll be in Jersey and the cops can't touch me. But when I got on the Verazano Bridge there were, like, thirty cop cars waiting there for me. So that's it, I pull over and I'm ready to go in peacefully. By that point I was tired of the whole thing. So, when I get outta the car, I got my hands on my head, like they do on TV, and I'm just standing there. Well this one cop who's supposed to put the cuffs on me—I'll never forget his name—O'Reilly, that Irish bastard—sorry your Honor. He comes up to me and starts pushing me, calling me a piece of garbage, saying he wishes he could just beat me till I'm senseless. Well I know my rights. I don't have to sit there taking that from some cop. So I yelled back at him. And then—I don't know, it depends on how you interpret it—I kinda may have pushed him, I think. See, he was so close to my face, with his bad breath and all. I just wanted a little breathing room. Problem is—and everything was happening so fast, you know—I may have instinctively, like, put out my hands, you know? Just to get that breathing room. And, well, when I put my hands out—I don't know—my fists, well, they couldda been closed. And I think that, well, um, my closed hands, they were, like, near his face. So,

63

I don't know, I guess to some of them, from their angle, it could have looked like I was punching him in the face—which I wasn't, technically. But I think the Irish bastard cop—sorry your Honor— I think he thought I punched him, because he went down like he was shot. *(Beat.)*

No, your Honor. Absolutely not! I did not deck him! See, his face kind of lunged forward right into my closed hands, which were just trying to get me a little breathing room. *(Beat.)*

Yeah, your Honor, that's what happened. The way it really happened, no matter what the cops say. So okay, now you know the story, I'm happy. And to be honest with you, your Honor, I kinda don't care at this point what you decide, because, I'm already in jail. Solitary confinement in my head, constantly think-ing, "how did I fuh—mess—it up so bad?" My wife, my kid, my family, her family, they pleaded, they yelled, and now they're done with me. I'm alone here, your Honor. With my brain racing all the time and me stuck in neutral, running outta gas. *(Beat.)*

Yeah, that's it, your Honor. You do what you got to do. I appreciate your letting me take a little time here. And I hope I helped clear up a few things. Thanks. Thanks a lot.

Liquid Healing
Mark Donnelly

Scene: here and now

Dramatic
Tim McCoy: Bitter and blind. 20s

> *Tim is haunted by the loss of his sight and the loss of his love.*
> *Here, he reveals the depths of his despair.*

(Tim McCoy, a blind man in his mid 20s, walks on stage. He
turns off the light switch on the wall and the lights dim so he
is somewhat in shadow. He struggles to find a chair, hits it as
he walks, curses, then gropes and finds the chair arm. He sits
down facing audience.)

TIM: There. Now we're all in the dark. *(Pause.)* How'd I get like
this? A fight, man. Fuckin' gang kids. Fourth of July…Bang…I
was going to pick up Molly, then drive us out to Jones Beach to
watch the fireworks with some friends. *(Pause.)* Fireworks, all
right. I'm coming out of the liquor store and I see these punks
breaking into my car. One of these creeps got a coat hanger and
he's shimmying it through the window to get the door button
up…I had an older car…'83 Cutlass. And this asshole's just about
got it open…like a game in a penny arcade where you use the little crane to extract the prize.

There's three of these guys, but I don't give a fuck. I snap. I
drop my shopping bag I'm so pissed…and the sixpack of
Michelob and the soda all smash on the ground. I go after the
guy with the hanger and grab his arm. And one of his pals jumps
me. Then Coat Hanger pokes me in the left eye. The bastard. I'm
screaming and I've got blood all over me. The punks just left me
there lying on the pavement. The store owner comes out…Asian
man. I gotta be grateful to him. He ripped his sport shirt off and

rapped it around my face. Got me down to the emergency room with his son driving like a madman. *(Pause.)*

The doctor couldn't save my eye. And here's the kicker. I end up eventually going blind in the right eye, too, because I'm diabetic. My father died of it when I was twelve. Then the diabetes started working on me at about twenty. Six months or so after the fight, that right eye was acting up…my vision got cloudier and cloudier…I was in my third year at St. John's. *(Pause.)* By the end of the spring semester I could barely see the print in my textbooks. I was using a magnifying glass, then even that wasn't helping. I walked out of my Business Management final. Couldn't read the charts and graphs for shit. *(Pause.)* That summer the doctor told me my diabetes made the deterioration in the other eye irreversible. I dropped out when that eye went and I was completely blind. *Lights out* for old Tim McCoy…only I'm still here walking around…just barely…Yeah, that trip to the frig for more beers is a killer… *(Pause.)* You know what I miss? I miss going into the kitchen in the dark late at night and letting the light from the frig brighten up the room just a little… *(As if talking to the inside of the refrigerator.)* No more Mr. Bright Guy now, you little light. You still working? Still amazing millions of other drunks with your late night bath of artificial sunshine? *(Pause. Speaks directly to audience again.)* Didn't know I was such a sensitive, literary bastard, did you? That's what an education can do for you. *(Pause.)* Oh, I tried to go back to college again to finish up. Had a counselor for the handicapped there who tried to help me with Braille. But that's tough. I think it's almost easier if you're blind as a kid. He also told me there's some kind of stuff you can do on the computer that's voice activated. Said there's all sorts of support groups for blind people…I know all that now. I went to one of those groups. The people even kid around, call themselves Blinks. But I'm not laughing. I felt uncomfortable around them. *(Pause.)* I'm getting disability checks from the Government. Even had money to pay for readers when I was still taking courses. Molly did some of it, but she'd never take the money. So I also got other readers through her…Molly was an elementary education major and some of her classmates were up for that kind of work…They didn't know what they were in for with me though. I gave 'em hell, I just was so frustrated and pissed off. I gave up altogether and never finished my degree. *(Pause.)* I'm not doing much now…unless you call smoking and drinking doing something. *(Pause.)* …My hobby? I watch TV…I mean, listen to TV…and get loaded. *(Lights a cigarette and smokes it.)*

They tell me all the smoking and drinking is bad for me. My mother is worried I'll fall asleep with a lit cigarette and burn the house down. *(Pause.)* I don't blame her. She works hard all day and comes home to find me in my sweats. Some days I don't even bother to take a shower. *(Pause.)* Where am I? Living in the house I grew up in and blind as a fuckin' bat. Talk about feeling like the baby brother! *(Pause.)* My sister Susan…she's a nurse. She comes by, but she's busy with her little boy. And my brother Bobby, he brings me out to his place on Long Island some weekends. It's better in the summer because he has a small motorboat he takes out into the Sound. He likes to get out there, says it clears his head from all the bullshit he sees as a New York City cop. But do you know how much you miss when you're out there on the water and you're blind? Sure, I can smell the salt, and put my hand in the water, and feel the sun…but *I can't see any of it*…I gotta rely on my memories of all that stuff…and they fade, man…really fade. *(Pause.)* Bobby's got a girlfriend named Marie. And they're gettin' married next year. Where's that put me? Mr. Third Wheel? *(Pause.)* Not this guy. I don't want it… *(Pause.)* I mentioned Molly already. I met her at St. John's before all this shit happened to me. Beautiful girl…Great girl…too great…stuck by me through all of this…Said it didn't matter if I was blind. Said she loved me, man and still wanted to marry me…we' d talked about that seriously before the accident…accident my ass. That bastard should have his own eyes gauged out man. *Fuck him.* *(Pause.)* Sometimes I wake up at night from dreams where I've thrown acid in his face…then destroyed the bastard by ripping his arms and legs off…Molly said I've got so much rage that's still inside me…that's what all the nutso drinking's about…I yell and scream at everybody…my family, friends…and Molly. She tried to calm me…tried to get me to talk to a therapist. I went a couple of times, but it didn't change anything. Didn't reduce the rage. Why wouldn't I be in a goddamn rage! What am I gonna do, rot in this house the rest of my life? *(Pause.)* I'd be at Molly's apartment and we'd make love. I'd be touching her body, so soft and smooth…and she would hold me close…but I couldn't see her…I couldn't see her face anymore, and look in her eyes when I'd be in her. *(Sadder.)* Never can again… *(Pause.)* I pushed her…I pushed her…I made things so ugly for her…I think it was intentional now. I couldn't bear her leaving me someday. I couldn't believe anybody could love me so much, put up with so much to stay with a blind guy. So I pushed her out the door…How else?…What else? It's hard man…I love her, but I don't want to be pitied. I don't want to be a charity case for her. *(Pause.)* What kind of job am I gonna get? A vocational counselor told me that with my intelligence and skills there were plenty of opportunities for me. Opportunities my ass! You know anybody who wants a blind office manager? Blind stock broker? And skills?…What skills! *(Pause.)* I never did know what the hell I wanted. Used to dream of flying planes when I was a kid. My grandfather flew in World War II. But when he died, my dream sort of died, too…And did you ever hear of a blind pilot? *(Pause.)* Molly's teaching at an elementary school out in Glen Cove. She's good with kids she's got patience…I'm probably the biggest kid she had to deal with…drove me to campus after I got hurt…Didn't matter if her classes weren't lined up with mine. She worked around it…she went all out for me…wouldn't give up on me…but I made it too rough for her…And now she's gone.

The Mayor Of Casterbridge

Philip Goulding
Adapted from the novel by Thomas Hardy

Scene: the nineteenth century village of Casterbridge, England

Dramatic
Henchard: a man coming to terms with the misdeeds of his past.
40–50

> *Henchard enjoys his life as mayor of this industrious little farming town and is planning to marry. When he is confronted by a woman he once wronged, he knows that he must do right by her as he here explains to a young friend.*

HENCHARD: A man makes mistakes, Farfrae, and I've never been a man to say I'll stick with just the one. While on business in Jersey one autumn I were took sinful ill. Twas the gloom took hold, on account of the loneliness of my domestic life I suppose. A man is due those times, is he not, when the world seems to have the blackness of hell, and like Job, he'll curse the very day that give him birth?

[FARFRAE: I have to say I've never felt that way.]

HENCHARD: Then pray to God you never may. For twas while I lay abed a lady took pity on me, and nursed me through. Don't ask me why, I'll not deny I was never worth her trouble. But she were warm all the same, and we got close. A scandal then arose which did me no harm but ruined her. When well enough again, I went away. She suffered, that I know, for she did write many times and tell me so—till I'd recently resolved to make things right atween us. You see now my dilemma Farfrae, for as it stands I must disappoint one of these two. And tis plain as day it's to Susan my allegiance must be due.

Moonlight Cocktail

Steven Keyes

Scene: Iota, East Texas

Serio-Comic
Bobby Don Flowers ("B.D."): a man sharing a memory of his father. 20s–30s

Watching a friend eat fortune cookies brings back memories for B.D. that aren't that happy.

B.D.: "Fortunes improve with time," huh?…My Dad'd love you.

[PATSY: Yer Dad?]

B.D.: …He loved fortunes, too? *(He takes ketchup bottle and slaps the base.)*

[PATSY: What? What about him?]

B.D.: He kept this big jar on a shelf in the basement, full of the fortunes from chinese cookies. From the only chinese restaurant in East Texas and the only restaurant we ever ate out in. Every Thursday. Like clockwork. I think it reminded him of the war. He loved the war. He always talked about it. I think that was the only time he was happy…He's gone.

[PATSY: I'm sorry.]

B.D.: I don't know where he went. He got out of here—he sure did. I haven't seen him since. I was ten. After he left, I used to come home every day from school, take that jar down, dump those fortunes on the rug and just look at them. There must have been hundreds. I looked on maps and in bus station windows. On trains that went past along the highway. But he was never there. Then one day, on the six o'clock news, I saw him. It was a special bulletin about a tornado in Port Arthur that had come and gone in five minutes but "left devastation in it's wake." People were crying, holding babies and walking on their houses. And there was my Dad, hosting with a microphone. I called the station and told them that my father had a son and to come home right away. I told them I was sure. They hung up twice. So, I took a bus downtown to KLIF-TV the next day while my Mom was at work and told them I'd wait to see my father. They asked me questions and gave me an ice cream cone. Finally, I saw him coming down the hallway. I was happy but he looked mad…The next day, we were both on the front page of the paper. I was "ROOKIE NEWS-MAN'S LOVE-CHILD."…Brad Kennedy wasn't my Dad, though, and I got grounded with no T.V. for a month and after awhile when my mother and I went into the chinese restaurant, the waiters and busboy stopped asking "Where Fodder?"

Murmurs of California

Robert Vivian

Scene: an upscale restaurant

Dramatic
Eliot: a dreamer longing for greatness. 30s

> *Eliot's pursuit of a career as a writer has led to the neglect of everything else in his life including his marriage. When his wife accuses him of stealing money from her from time to time, he acknowledges his petty theft.*

ELIOT: I go into the bedroom while you're still sleeping and look for the envelope next to the shoe rack. It looks like it's been trampled in a stampede. I take it out and count the cash. Carefully. Carefully. It's always stuffed with twenties. There you are sleeping like an angel with your beautiful black hair all tossed up on the pillow, and I quietly take an Andrew Jackson. I put Andy in my pocket. He slips in like a key into a lock. And then I just stand there. I can't even hear you breathe. The room is so still. It's like winter in the room, with the moon out. You are the moon. I feel such incredible tenderness for you. I swear I'm going to make it up to you. I don't know how, but I will, Kate. I promise. I go to you and kiss you on your forehead. You're a cool moon, but warm. Warm and cool. The perfect moon temperature. What are you dreaming? I tuck the blanket around your sleeping shoulders. I don't want to go. I don't want to get in that car and drive away. I don't want to teach. I don't want to go into that stupid classroom and pretend I have something to say. I've said and felt all I need to say before the sun even came up, before you were even awake.

Murmurs of California

Robert Vivian

Scene: an upscale restaurant

Dramatic
Eliot: a dreamer longing for greatness. 30s

> *Eliot's wife and father share a sudden impulsive desire to drive to California. Here, Eliot reveals the face of the inertia that is preventing him from going anywhere, let alone California.*

ELIOT: For a long time now…For maybe my whole life, in fact…I've wanted to see the face of God. I know it's crazy. I know it sounds off the point. But I can't see him. Don't you understand? He doesn't show up anywhere. He's not at parties. He's not in the closet. He doesn't visit me when I'm in the bathtub floating all by myself. I go for long walks in the neighborhood, and I pick up branches and twigs in the gutters. Just to see…Just to…alleviate the pain. *(Pause.)* He's not there. So I've started to climb this mountain. It's a mountain I've made up in my head. But it's so real. The rocks are real. They smash my feet. The slope is real. I'm climbing toward God. I'm taking it step by step, I'm out of breath, I lean my head against a pine tree that is leaning out toward the horizon. Beetles climb across my forehead and I brush them off. I can't bring myself to kill them. Maybe before but not now. Now I'm likely to put them in my pocket and set them down later in a safe place, far away from harm *(Silence. He looks at them.)* I'm not saying it's normal or right or even makes sense. I'm not saying any of those things. Only…I use words to help me get up the mountain. These are not normal words but words with spikes on them, with little studs that dig into the side of the mountain.

Office Hours

Norm Foster

Scene: the office of a TV news producer

Serio-Comic
Warren: a bitter news reporter, 40s

> *Warren has reported the news for twenty-three years and has recently been demoted to covering fluff stories by Pam, a brash young producer who rubs him the wrong way. Here, he waits in Pam's office and prepares to tell her exactly what he thinks of her.*

WARREN: You twit. You inarticulate, BMW-driving, tofu-eating twit. *(Beat.)* No, that might be too confrontational. Uh…All right, let's try this. You know something, Ms. Gerard? Mrs. Gerard? Pam? Can I call you Pam, Pam? No, the more I say it, the more it sounds like Spam. Pamela, I'm given to understand that you don't like my work. No, too civil. Be a little more intimidating. Give it the Robert DeNiro inflection. You got a problem with my work? Are you serious? You can't be serious. My work? Are you tellin' me you got a problem with my work? No. Okay, start off with a joke. All right. All right. Pam, don't you think it's funny that my name is Warren Kimble and yours is Pam Gerard? Huh? Kimble, Gerard? We've got kind of a "Fugitive" thing happening here. Kind of a David Janssen, Barry Morse kind of thing. No, screw the jokes. Get right to the point Pam, I get the feeling that you don't like my work. Well, right now, honey, I don't like my work either. And I'll tell you why. I'm a news reporter, Pam. I've been working my way up for twenty-three years. That's right. Some of us work our way up. We don't marry the station manager and go from television bingo hostess to news producer just like that. But, that doesn't bother me. No, that doesn't bother me one goddamned bit. What bothers me is that I was the top reporter in this city at one time, I did stories with integrity. Stories I was proud of. And now? Two weeks ago I covered a wake for a racehorse. What the hell is that?! So the horse died. Who gives a shit? It's not Black Beauty for Godssake. And last week you sent me to interview that Pentecostal group that wants to put a loin cloth on the statue of Cupid. So, there I am interviewing the queen of the tight-asses while Cupid urinates into a fountain behind me. How in the hell am I supposed to do good work in a situation like that, you slack-jawed, addle-brained, Melrose Place-watching, harpy. I need the hard-hitting—stories. And I'm not talking about doing "Death Of A Salesman" every night. Just something newsworthy. That's all I ask. I mean, hell, I'm forty-eight years old. I've got a mortgage I'm paying off and a kid I'm trying to put through university. That's a school, Pam. A big one with people your age in it—but, I'd sooner be out of work than do the crap stories you're giving me. So, that's it. That's all I have to say. And if you want to fire me, you go right the hell ahead because, quite frankly, lady, I don't give a tinker's toot. Oh, and one more thing. I don't appreciate being summoned into your office like one of your underlings and then being left here to ponder my fate while you get called away on some petty emergency. You understand what I'm saying, you scrotum-cracking, Alanis Morrisette-loving, preening little tart! Warren Kimble waits for no one!

The Passion Play

Gabriel Lanci

Scene: a restaurant

Dramatic

Young Man: an embittered young man confronting his estranged father. 20–30

> *Jack has found the man he believes to be his father. Here, he tells the sad and terrifying story of the night he was abandoned by his father in a bus terminal.*

YOUNG MAN: I remember my father—can you believe that? I was only four, maybe five, when he left. I remember him taking me downtown to the bus terminal and having me sit on a bench in the waiting room, and then he left. When he came back I didn't recognize him, he was changed—and this is strange—he looked more like my father than he had before.

[MAN: The man who took you to the bus terminal wasn't your father.]

YOUNG MAN: How do you know? He was my father. They were the same person. But something had happened to him—his clothes were different. His whole character was different. How can a kid five years old know that?

[MAN: You were probably right. Children are closer to their instincts. What was different about your father?]

YOUNG MAN: I'd never seen him before like that. I didn't believe he was my father at first. I remember him trying to talk to me, I must have cried or looked frightened or something. I knew he was my father, the change was so sudden, his appearance was a shock.

[MAN: What was it that shocked you?]

YOUNG MAN: It came to me a few years ago…he'd shaved off his beard! My father had this beard that covered half his face. I remember him holding me as a kid, how it used to pinch and scratch when he kissed me. Sometimes when he held me on his lap he used to brush it across the top of my head to tease me. And there he was, revealed to me that day in the terminal—he'd been hiding all those years. He had a key on a cord and he put this around my neck and said, don't lose this. I can even remember his voice when he said it. And then he went away. I never saw him again.

[MAN: What do you mean, you never saw him again?]

YOUNG MAN: He left. He just walked off and left me in the terminal. I was sitting there alone in the bus terminal for hours. I started walking around and someone asked me if I was lost. I think I cried and this woman brought me to a cop who took me to the stationhouse. They couldn't get anything out of me. I was waiting for my father, waiting and waiting. I believed he was coming back for me, and they had taken me away. He would return and be worried. *(Laughs.)* Can you believe it! I was worried about him.

[MAN: What happened to you?]

YOUNG MAN: They noticed the key and sent someone to the locker at the terminal. It contained my father's clothes and a note telling them who I was and where I lived. Then they called my mother and she came and got me.

The Passion Play

Gabriel Lanci

Scene: a restaurant

Dramatic
Young Man: an embittered young man confronting his estranged father. 20–30

> *Here, the young man reveals that he has been secretly watching his father for some time.*

YOUNG MAN: I worked once as a harvester cutting down old stalks and binding them up. It was a field you had planted, father. Did you know I was working for you? It amused me that you might not know.

[MAN: I knew.]

YOUNG MAN: The first time I worked the field a hawk flew over my head, it followed me day after day, waiting for me to pass by. My cutting exposed the earth and the small life that lived beneath the stalks—waiting, not coming near until I had passed. Then I would hear behind me the rush of wings, a falling out of the sky, and sometimes a small, painful cry, the rush of air again and then—silence. I would be alone for a few minutes, and then he'd be back. Watching, waiting for me to pass on and expose his prey. I thought, how like father he is. Watching, waiting for me to move on, always waiting. Those eyes watching me, separating me from the earth and the prey he seeks. Waiting for me, the harvester, the instrument of his hunt. *(Pause.)* What the hawk does is cruel, but he lives by it. It doesn't seem cruel to him. Does the mouse know this? How did the mole reason, and the young rabbit that cried out in pain? You made them what they are in that field. Did they know you?

[MAN: Like the two men at the bar, no.]

YOUNG MAN: They were only imperfect in your perfect world.

Poona the Fuckdog, and Other Plays for Children

Jeff Goode

Scene: the faraway land of myth and allegory

Serio-Comic
Shrub: a passionate plant. Any age

> *Here, a militant shrub reveals the genesis of his desire to change the world.*

SHRUB: When I was in shrub school, one of my professors, a withered old bush with gnarly arms like a Japanese banzai, stood in front of the class and asked us: "Why shrubbery?" "What is the role of the shrub in society?" Well, we were all idealistic young seedlings, and at that question, a dozen branches shot up. And we began shouting our answers. One young fir wanted to "challenge" his audience. Another thought shrubbery should educate. But I had them all beat, because I wanted to change the world. I wanted people to walk into a garden where I was playing a hedge, and walk out of that garden ready to grab injustice in their fists and crush it into dust. But before I could speak, the teacher suddenly cut us off. Not literally. He cut us off, and he said: "The role of the shrub is to enlighten. That is the most you can do. Nobody ever came out of an orchard a new man. Nobody ever looked at a beautiful landscape and felt compelled to overthrow a government. Or write a law. Or write a letter." The old bush folded his limbs across his trunk, and smiled at us, "Enlighten, my children."

That day changed my life. Because I look at all the gardens around me—professional gardens! and I realize…he was right. Here was one of the great shrubs of his day. A bush who had

79

worked with *Ming Cho Lee!!* And *he* never changed the world. The great shrubs of our day never changed the world.

Because they never even tried.

Because they sit with their limbs folded across, saying: "Enlighten, my children. And someday you can aspire to be as great as the grizzled old growth who squats before you. Enlighten, and you, too, may blossom into a very reputable stump. With tenure."

And I said, "Fuck this fertilizer!" I *will* change the world. I will prune myself until people look at me. And die. They will look at me. And find God. They will look at me. And walk out of that garden and down the block and rush into a burning building to save a child. And some of them will look at me and write a letter. Or write a law. Or plant a tree.

And if I fail. If it *is* impossible.

Well, flying was impossible. But *somebody* had to put wings on that bicycle.

Poona the Fuckdog, and Other Plays for Children
Jeff Goode

Scene: the faraway land of myth and allegory

Serio-Comic
God: an omnipotent deity. Any age

> *When questioned about his divine plan, God makes the following reply.*

GOD: You want to know what's the divine plan?
 [(Jack puts down the five bucks.)]
GOD: Couple years ago. Or maybe it was a couple million, I lose track. A seventy-two foot long diplodocus walks in here. You know what that is right, diplodocus? Walks in here, says, "God, what's the divine plan? I mean, here I'm trying to be good, do the right thing, I go to church, give money to the poor, give money to the church, build a church. So I can die and go to heaven. That's how it works, right? That's where I fit into the divine plan right?" And you know what I said to this diplodocus? No, you don't. Because you are not all seeing and all knowing like me. I said to this diplodocus: Here's the plan. You live, you do whatever, good bad ugly, I don't give a fuck, because the whole time you're living, and your grandchildren, and every diplodoci after you. there's these little rats runnin' around in the muck evolving. Turning into cats and dogs and monkeys. And some of those monkeys are gonna ask themselves the same question: "What should I do with my life? What's my place in the divine plan?" And the whole time they're doing that, and evolving, and building hockey rinks and microcomputers. There's these little bugs called cockroaches runnin' around in the muck. And they're evolving. And the computers are evolving.

And later after the hockey rinks are all gone, the cockroaches are gonna ask me the same thing, and the computers: "What should I do with my life? How do I get to heaven?" And after the cockroaches come these things that there ain't even a name for, yet. But they're cute as heck, and they mix a mean margarita. And they're gonna get together with the neo-computers—is what they'll be called—and they are gonna create this *new* race of creatures. And *they*...

...I don't know what they're going to do.

...And I'm looking forward to that.

Poor, Pathetic Will

Terryl Paiste

Scene: London, 1588

Serio-Comic
A Horse-holder. 50–70

> *This dedicated horse-holder takes great pride in his profession. Here, he tells the tale of a failed young horse-holder who fancied himself a playwright.*

> *(An energetic senior stands on an empty stage, looking around for a potential customer. He spots one.)*

HORSE-HOLDER: Hold on to your horse for you, sire? Half a farthing! Only half a— *(Watches customer walk away. He shrugs philosophically, then notices the audience.)* Oh, I know what you're thinking. I hear it every day. "What's a fellow your age doing out in the street, hanging on to the reins of horses for a living? This is 1588! Time to rest by the fire, let the young folks have a turn!" *(Shakes head.)* They mean well, but they don't understand. Me, I've sailed the seas with Sir Francis Drake himself. Had a turn at the greengrocer's trade, too. And if there's one thing I've learned—well, two things—it's that London is world enough for a proper man. And the greengrocer's trade is dull. But horses? *(Wags finger at audience.)* The wave of the future! And it's fond of horses, I am. Not like the young lads what take the job just to earn a shilling or two until something 'better' comes along. *(Looks around to make sure he won't be overheard.)* That chap, Will, for instance. Stands outside the theater every day, holding on to horses for the gentry, but his heart's not in it. Wants to be a playwright, he says. Always daydreaming about his stories and not paying proper attention to the horse. Gives the rest of us a bad name. *(Earnestly.)* "Will," I says to him, "You've got to be more ambitious if you want to make your mark in the big city. Do what I did! Put a bit aside every week, and one of these days you'll have enough to open your own stable, too. The first horse, that's the hardest to come by. Oh, I gave my kingdom for that first horse of mine, and worth every penny she was." *(Shrugs.)* But Will wasn't listening. Scratching down words with that quill pen he was, instead of looking after his horse. Pathetic.

A fortnight ago, he tried to get me to read one of his plays. I explained to him, kindly like, because he's only four-and-twenty, too young to know any better—I told him straight off I didn't hold with wasting time reading. Oh, I can write my own name and read my prayers in chapel, but what's the good of books when there's money to be made tending horses?

So he starts in telling me the story of his play, and since business was slow, I had no choice but to listen. And I almost fell asleep, so boring it was. Two young lovers, but their families were bitter enemies. Same old plot we've all heard a million times. But wait. It gets worse. What does Will do with these star-crossed lovers? He has them run off together and live happily ever after. Even my horse yawned.

"That scene on the balcony's not bad," I told him. (Truth be told, I thought it was slow, but I was trying to spare his feelings. I'm tenderhearted that way.) "And the nurse character is worth a chuckle, maybe even a laugh. But let's face it, Will, you need more action! More drama! The ladies will never go for that happy ending. Tears, that's what the ladies like. And a dead body when the curtain goes down, preferably two."

He nods, all thoughtful like, and I figured that was the end of it, and good riddance. But no. The next day, he's telling me his *other* stories. What should he do to perk up his Scottish play? "Bring on some witches," I say. "Everybody likes witches." *(Speaks in Will's tentative tone.)* "And the one about the Prince of Denmark?" *(In his granddaughter's voice, confident.)* "Start out with a ghost," my little granddaughter tells him. She'd brought me my mid-day meal and stayed to offer her opinion, which Will was grateful to hear. He was desperate for ideas, poor chap.

But by the end of the day, I was beginning to lose patience. Especially with the plot of the eleventh play. "You've got a ship in the middle of a tempest," I tell him. "Isn't it obvious what you should do? SINK THE SHIP! SINK THE SHIP!"

"Of course," he says, slapping his forehead. "Why didn't I think of that?"

By that point I'd had enough. I mean, I was standing there, knee-deep in mud, holding the reins for *both* our horses. At least, I *hope* it was mud. This couldn't go on.

"Will," I says, "You're a good bloke, but you've got to make up your mind. Either you're going to settle down to a serious career as a horse-handler and get rich some day, or you're doomed to waste your time with these plays and end up a failure. You can't do both." Stern talk, I know, especially coming from one so much more successful, but it was for his own good. Someday he'd thank me.

"You're right," he says. "You're always right. What should I do?"

"I can't tell you that," I says. (Actually, I could, but I was tired of doing the lad's thinking for him.) "But I'll give you a hint. Something my grandfather used to say. 'This above all. To thine own self be true.'"

I haven't seen Will around much lately. To tell you the truth, I kind of miss the young scalawag. But I don't think he had it in him to be a playwright. And certainly not a handler of horses, which is much more difficult. Not to mention, useful.

Still, I gave him my best advice, and that's all we can do for the ignorant young, isn't it? Pass along our wisdom. And who knows? Mayhap my grandmother was thinking of some poor scamp like Will when she used to say, "All's well that ends— *(He spots a customer.)* Well, a customer! Hold your horse for you, sire? *(Exits, chasing after customer.)* Half a farthing! Only half a farthing!

Prelude To Pizza

Jeff Goode

Scene: here and now

Serio-Comic
A Philosophical Pizza Delivery Guy. 20s–30s

> *Here a hungry customer gets more than he or she ordered from a loquacious pizza delivery guy.*

DELIVERY GUY: You gotta always remember to don't blame the messenger.

Cuz it's like the Virgin Mary of the Freezer. Remember her? I knew her I mean the lady that found her. I didn't see the Virgin Mary in person till later when she was on TV. She was the mother of a friend of mine, his cousin. And she thought she saw the Virgin Mary in the condensation on a freezer door at Quik Trip. They showed it on TV. It was just this, ya know, condensation, and it was kinda Virgin Mary shaped if you look at it. What's the word for that? Madonnic? Kinda curved like a woman with a shawl over her head. Peanut-shaped is, I guess, the word I'm lookin' for. Or like half a snowman. And these spikes around it from how the frost sorta crystallized and froze. So it looked like she was glowing. So, like a radioactive peanut. Or the Virgin Mary. Anyway, she discovered this vision. And they put it on TV. And she took it as a sign from God that it was okay for Marco to be gay. That's her son. My friend's cousin. And also that she should play the lottery. So since then, his whole family's been very supportive of his life style. And they play the powerball. So it's great that she was able to take something away from her experience with the freezer door at Quik Trip. But it's still a freezer door. I mean, it still is. They didn't frame it or anything. Somebody wiped it down, so you can't see the Virgin Mary any more. But it's still there, keeping the Hagen Dasz warm. And that's pretty much all it set out to do in the first place. And that's like me. I swear the way people treat me sometimes, you'd think I was a door to door salesman for Jehovah's Witness. Believe me, if something jumps out of here and saves your soul, I will be as surprised as you. Cuz it's never done that before. I don't think my insurance would cover if I was driving around with a seatful of salvation.

Prelude To Pizza

Jeff Goode

Scene: here and now

Serio-Comic
A Philosophical Pizza Delivery Guy. 20s–30s

> *Here a hungry customer gets more than he or she ordered from a loquacious pizza delivery guy.*

DELIVERY GUY: The closest I ever came was one time I was making a delivery down over on…Fuck. Why can't I remember street names? Well, anyway, what the point is, I was making a delivery and I rang the door and it got all quiet. Cuz before I could hear yelling and hitting and stuff, and I rang the door and *nothing*.

And then this big guy came to the door. Opened the door. Bright red in the face and sweaty. And he's breathing kinda heavy, like he's gonna have a heart attack. So, of course, right away my first thought is I'm thinking: This guy is thirsty. So I asked if he'd like a liter of soda pop with that. Cuz that's one of the things we're allowed to do is suggestive sell on the soda pop. Which they send us out with extra just in case. And you can even, if you go to the bulk store, buy your own and sell them that and make a little extra that way if you don't report it. And it's pure profit. Except for what you pay for the pop, and gas and anything else you buy.

But I don't do that anymore because of one summer it was really hot and so I got some cases of root beer the night before, just in case. And the next day when I was at my daytime job at the Walmart, it was 103 degrees in the parking lot and it exploded all over the back of my Chevette. Not the parking lot. But the root beer. And I had to sell the car after that.

Oh! Because I guess this was that night because he said: "What? What do I look like?" The guy. And I said—and I wasn't just saying this—honest to God, he looked like a guy who could really use some root beer. So that's what I said. And he just started *laughing*. And kinda in my face. And I know you're not supposed to do this. But something came over me. And I looked at him and I said: "It's just ninety-nine cents each...Damn you." Which, that made him laugh even harder. But now, I felt like he was laughing with me, not at me. And he said, "Okay. Get my wallet, bitch."

I guess that's what he called her. Because this woman, or his girlfriend, or whatever she was got up from sitting on the kitchen floor and wiped her eyes and went in the other room to get the money. So I went back out to the car.

And that's when I saw how all the root beers had exploded over the back of my car. Because the pizza rides up front. So I hadn't even checked. And I was just...You know how when it's hot? And, like, you got root beer all over your upholstery. And you make minimum wage, and you drive a Chevette, and I just broke one of the cardinal rules of suggestive selling, which is...Don't say, "It's just ninety-nine cents, damn you" to the customer. And he laughed in your face...and I just started crying right there in the driveway.

And the woman, the guy's woman came out of the house with money for the pizza and the root beer. And she put her hand on my shoulder, and she said...I don't remember. Something like..."Here's your money." And I was gonna say "I'm sorry, I don't have any root beer," but when I looked up at her, I could see that she was pretty beat up. Y'know, like when somebody beats the shit out you. And she had a black eye. And I looked at her and I said..."I'm sorry, I don't have any root beer."

And she kinda went "Oh," like, ya know, when you don't know what else to say. And sort of stood there looking at the money like she didn't know what to do and you could tell she'd taken the time to get the exact change, which was eleven something, because of the coupon.

So that's when I said, "Are you okay?" And then she laughed. And she said "No." Then she handed me the money, even the two dollars for the root beer and turned around and went back into the house. When she closed the door I could still hear the guy was laughing. And she was laughing. And I thought, ya know, if I hadn't come along right when I did with the pizza. And theoretically with two liters of root beer. And brought laughter into that house for one minute…he might have really hurt her, or something, or killed her.

Which is what eventually happened a couple days later from what I read in the paper. At least, the address was the same. Which, I guess I forgot to mention before, is why I had to sell the car. Not from the root beer. *(Pause.)* …I don't know why I tell that story.

Red Breams

Linda Stockham
Poetry by Lanny Fields

Scene: the solarium of an isolated house by the ocean, Spring, 1996

Dramatic
William Francis DeMissie: the ghostly presence of a poet who has recently committed suicide. 60–90

> *A young freelance journalist has traveled quite a distance to interview the reclusive DeMissie, who unfortunately took his own life the night before her arrival. Here, his unhappy spirit reveals the depth of guilt that had forced him to agree to the interview.*

DEMISSIE: *(Harshly; perhaps he says it brutally.)* I am the product of deception, and you are my child—

[PAULA: I do not understand—]

DEMISSIE: *(Quickly cutting her off; he speaks with fiery contempt.)* Passion and jealousy, my dear, are the grounds of great pain. End both and you end the desire to create. My Mother was a beautiful woman but she was corrupt. She was as corrupt as that portrait-painter cousin of hers, Lyle Cornwell. Ha! His only claim to fame was to have drowned off the coast of northwestern Italy like Shelley. He teased her with that model, whom both desired. I was seventeen. I adored her in spite of her weaknesses…I wrote the poetry because I needed to release the pain in some constructive way. Then, it all became too much for me. One night I took them both. Took them as brutally as I could. As brutally as a frightened and yet angry seventeen year old would who knew no other way of fighting back. Lyle took the model away. She wrote my Mother seven months later from Genoa to say she was pregnant. She didn't answer him. You see, she was pregnant, too. I

91

had planted my seeds in both. And both had daughters. One daughter was Mrs. Hallett's mother, the other was your grandmother. You and Mrs. Hallett are of my blood! My children! My heirs! *(A brief pause.)* Lyle wrote about the baby, and yet my Mother never wrote to tell him about hers. Dad, in his dullish way, took the babe away and gave it up for adoption. Mother went into the sea; she went into the sea to cleanse herself of the afterbirth she thought had never been expelled. That filthy, horrible looking flotsam! Death, death, death!

(Pulling away, and as he does, the lights come back up.)
DEMISSIE: "What is death? How tender, frail life:
Delicate orchid, butterfly wing, snail's
Horn, all aquiver before death's strife.
Gone, alone, sole bereft, yet my wails
Cannot return her to my embrace. Winter's
Sleety fury howls oer his lament, numb
Discern ignores the savage blasts. Splinter
Ice-shards arrow willow and beast dumb.
Awake Bard! Reach out to spring's succor
And seek her whose memory shrouds white
And bleak. Play the warming lyrics before
We perish, dance the orange, taste the night.
What is life? I must seek her, my being's repose,
And return her to the terrestrial realm, to trees,
Leas, and flowers of gold. What is life? Suppose
It's mere dream, fantasy's jest, then…O please."

Rockaway Boulevard

Richard Vetere

Scene: an apartment in Queens

Dramatic
Johnny Montenlli: a hard-working blue- collar guy. 30s

> *Faced with the harsh reality of having to provide care for his invalid father, Johnny here reminisces about happier times.*

JOHNNY: Why can't things be the way they used to?

[HELEN: Like what?]

JOHNNY: Like hangin' out with the guys on Friday night. Pickin' you up on Saturday, goin' down to the Bow Wow with everybody. You know, Ralphie, Tony the Face, Sheila and Joanne. Man, we used to have a good time. Fightin' the guys over in Far Rockaway, racin' the cars over the toll bridge. Remember that beat up Dodge I had? We'd be doin' that stuff right now, you know that? This time on Saturday night we'd be doin' that right now. You and me and everybody else. Eatin' breakfast at the diner, watchin' the sun come up, singing "Do wop a do," under the bridge just to hear the echo. Then we'd go to the beach on Sunday mornin' and sleep all day, get nice and tan. "Hey, Ralphie, come on, let's drive down to 116th Street. Sheila said the girls will meet under the boardwalk. Don't worry about nothin'. The sun is shining like a brand new watch! We got time. We got plenty of time. We got all summer."

[HELEN: Honey, that was ten years ago.]

JOHNNY: We should call some of those people. We used to have fun.

The Room Inside the Room I'm In

Simon Fill

Scene: a subway stop

Dramatic
Joe: a young man haunted by his brother's suicide. 20s

> *Joe has waited for four days in this subway stop hoping to find Essie, a friend from his past. When his vigil pays off, Joe tries to tell the surprised Essie what prompted him to search for her.*

JOE: Your brother kills himself and what's there to say 'cept it wasn't 'cause he...loved anyone. Two and a half years, like two and a half days. A few months ago I started to forget a little, and I saw you in a library. Asleep. In a quiet room. In a room inside the room I was in. I moved closer, and there was nothing. The air. And people still in their forgetfulness. And quiet. Quiet. When I looked closer, it wasn't you at all. But an old woman, like you might look old. She opened her eyes and looked at me. But she didn't know who I was. We didn't know each other. *(Beat.)* Rick's sister Amy told him she saw you in this neighborhood last week, with groceries. I needed to find you. It's incredible how boring a subway stop is over four days.

Sakina's Restaurant

Aasif Mandvi

Scene: an Indian restaurant

Serio-Comic
Azgi: an optimistic and energetic immigrant, Indian. 20s

> *Azgi has recently arrived in the USA from India. Here we find*
> *him waiting tables at Sakina's Restaurant.*

AZGI: ABDUL! I need two puri's on table five! I need two lassi's on
table six, and this lamb curry is COLD COLD, COLD! Food, Abdul,
is supposed to be HOT, HOT! Not COLD! How come you don't
seem to understand that????? *(Azgi runs to speak to one of his
tables. To first table.)* I am very sorry. In all the time that I have
worked in this restaurant, food is NEVER cold, NEVER! He is heat-
ing it up right now. I will bring it out in two minutes and you just
keep enjoying your...water. *(He moves to the second table.)*
Hello, how are you? My name is Azgi, I will be your waiter. How
can I help you? Oh yeah, it is kind of spicy, but we have a scale.
You see, you can order how spicy you would like one, two, three,
four, five. You decide, he'll make it.—What?—You want number
five? *(Azgi is a little concerned.)* Sir don't take number five, take
number two—No, no, number two is better for you, it's very
good, you'll like it very much.—Please sir, don't take number five.
Sir I am trying to save your life OK. *(Getting angry.)* look, look in
my eyes OK, number two is better for you. OK you think about it
I will come back OK. *(He runs upstage again.)* ABDUL!—Where is
my lamb curry ????

> *(The lamb curry seems to have appeared on the line.)*

AZGI: A-ha! *(He runs over to the first table with the imaginary
lamb curry. It is very hot and burns his hands.)* There you go. OK?
piping hot—What happened? Why you look so sad? Not
lamb?—CHICKEN.—Oh my God!—No, no, please sit down.

95

Where you going? please don't leave, sit down, I am very sorry, this is a terrible mistake, I will bring out chicken in just two minutes, please don't leave, whatever you do don't leave. *(He runs over to second table.)* OK, OK, look I tell you what, number three, number three is plenty hot, plenty hot. You don't need number five. LISTEN MAN!! I AM FROM INDIA!!! and even in India nobody asks for number five! It's not a real thing that you can eat, it's just for show. I am not screaming, you are screaming! Look, look, now your wife is crying! I didn't make her cry, you made her cry! OK, OK. Fine, Fine, you want five, fifteen, one hundred five!! I give you OK!

ABDUL!—- Listen on dup forty-one, I put number five, but you don't make it number five, you make it number two, OK? And this lamb curry is supposed to be chicken curry—Because I am telling you, that's why. Because I am the boss right now OK, Listen you give me any trouble no, I will have Mr. Hakim fire you!!!—Oh, yeah? Oh, yeah? Come on, Come on Abdul *(He puts up his fists.)* I will take you right now! I will kick your butt so hard that you will be making lamb curry for the tigers in India! Oh, yeah? Come on, Big Guy, come on, Big Guy, come on, Big Guy, come on—

(Suddenly Azgi is faced with Abdul who grabs him by the collar.)

AZGI: —BIG GUY! I am joking, man. I am just kidding around, why you take me so seriously?—please don't kill me. *(Turning.)* Every night I have the same dream. I am a giant tandoori chicken wearing an Armani suit. I am sitting behind the wheel of a speeding Cadillac. I have no eyes to see, no mouth to speak and I don't know where I am going. Mr. Hakim, he come up to me, he say, "Azgi, Azgi, Azgi, you have to calm down, man, he say to me, he say "Success, Azgi, is like a mountain. From far away it is inspiring, but when you get close, you realize that it is simply made of earth and dirt and rocks, piled one on top of the other until it touches the sky." Mr. Hakim, he is a smart man, but I wonder to myself when God was building the mountain and piling the rock, one on top of the other, was he working or playing? *(He begins to ponder this thought, and then suddenly he smiles and goes over to the first table.)* Hello, my name is Azgi...I am working...and playing. *(He goes over to the second table.)* Hello my name is Azgi, I am working and playing...how are you ? *(He goes over and looks in the direction of Abdul, and blows him a big kiss.)* ABDUL...I love you man!!!!

(Phone rings, Azgi turns and looks at the audience.)
AZGI: Phone! *(He picks up the phone.)* Hello, Sakina's Restaurant Azgi speaking, how may I—Oh Oh Mr. Hakim? No No He is right here, I will get him—

Sakina's Restaurant

Aasif Mandvi

Scene: an Indian restaurant

Serio-Comic
Ali: a young man visiting a prostitute. 20s

> *Ali must marry Sakina as their families have arranged.*
> *Unfortunately, he is in love with Karen. Here, Ali engages the*
> *services of a hooker hoping that he can have the fantasy of*
> *Karen since the real thing is forever forbidden to him.*

ALI: Shut Up!—Shut Up!—I have to walk, I have to clear my head, and I have to come back. I have to walk, I have to clear my head, I have to come back, I have to walk, I have to clear my head, I have to come back. I have to WALK! I have to clear my head, I have to come— *(Suddenly he looks up as if someone has opened a door and he is staring into their face. He is visibly nervous, his mouth is dry and his hands are sweaty.)* I only have fifty dollars, I don't know if that's enough or not. Oh, that's fine, whatever you do for fifty dollars is fine. I don't know if I want the complete package anyway. It's probably safer that way, in regards to diseases and such. *(Realizing his faux pas.)* I'm sorry, I'm not saying that you have any diseases. Oh no I ruined the mood. I'm sorry, its just that I'm a Pre-Med student, so I'm always thinking about diseases. I don't do this kind of thing normally—NEVER!! never before actually, I don't know if that matters to you, but it matters to me, and so I just thought I would share that with you. *(Pulling money out of his pocket and handing it to her.)* Look, I'll just give you the money and you can put it over there on the dresser, or in your— *(Noticing that she put it in her underwear.)* there!—This is very unlikely for me to be in a place like this,—I've actually been trying to deepen my religious faith lately. I'm a Muslim, you know. Do you know what that is?…Yes, it's a type of cloth. What is your name?—Angel?—Really? *(He laughs.)* No, no, I'm sorry. I was just thinking that that's an ironic name for someone who does what you do for a living.—What?—No, no, I'm sorry, I'm not a jerk. I'm sorry that was rude, look I think you're very attractive. In fact, that's even the reason I followed you in here from the street…was because of the way you look…or at least who you look like. Well, you see, you look amazingly like this girl Karen who sits next to me in my Human Anatomy class, and who I cannot stop thinking about, and earlier this evening I was trying to study for my exam tomorrow, but I can't seem to concentrate because I can't stop thinking about Karen, and then when I think about Karen all the time, I think about my parents beating their chests when they realize I've failed all my exams. So I decided to take a walk and pray for some concentration, and that's when I saw you, and you—well, you look exactly like her, and you looked at me, and you smiled, and so when you started walking I followed you, and while I was walking up the stairs just now to this little room, I started thinking to myself that you must be a sign…a sign from God!! that since I'll never be with Karen, I could be with you, and then I could go home and be able to study, and pass my exam and make my parents proud of me!!! *(He suddenly breaks down into tears.)* I'm sorry, I'm really sorry, I think I've made a terrible mistake. You see I just realized that God would never, never lead me to a place like this. I must be losing my mind. I have to study, I have to go! I need some sleep! I have to study, I'm really sorry. I have obviously wasted your time, I'm really sorry but I have to go. *(He leaves, there is a long pause and then he returns.)* I think I should probably just get a refund. I don't know what your policy is as far as refunds go. I'm sure that it doesn't come up very often.—What?—Uh, thank you, that's very kind of you—Well I think you're very attractive yourself—No, I can't do that actually, No I can't, No I really can't—Well, because I'm engaged…or at least "betrothed" which is actually more like…engaged!—She's a very nice girl, Sakina!! would you like to see a picture? I have one,—No of course not, What I'm trying to say is that she really is the perfect girl for me, comes from a very similar family, same religion, same tradition, same values, these things are important, you know. Besides, Karen is just a distraction. I mean, she's American. In the long run she would never accept Indian culture, she would never understand the importance of an Islamic way of life, she would probably want to have pre-marital sex which is something that as a Muslim I could never do. I know that that probably sounds ridiculous under the circumstances, but it's true!!! It's not just a religion you know, it's a way of life and I have dedicated my entire spiritual life identity to the complete submission to the will of God. That's what Islam means. So you see, I can't just be running around having sex *(He thrust his pelvis forward unconsciously.)* like a rabbit *(He does it again, with more vigour.)* with every woman I am attracted to *(He does it again repeatedly with real vigour.)* It would be SIN!! and that is why I have to leave. What? What is my name? *(He pauses.)* AL!— Really!—OK, OK. It's not Al the way you are thinking of it, like short for Alan or Alvin or something. It's actually the short form of a very religious name, a name I can't even say right now, otherwise it would be a sin—I think. I probably don't even deserve this name.

(We begin to hear the song "No Ordinary Love." This plays throughout the rest of the piece.)

ALI: What are you doing?—no I really don't think you should …REMOVE THAT!!! *(He hides behind his hands so as not to look at her but then he slowly looks.)* You want me to call you Karen?…OK!? Karen, Karen, Karen, Karen…

[(She unbuttons his pants and begins to perform oral sex, the rest of the lines are delivered while he is receiving a blow job.)]

ALI: Oh, my God, this is not me, this is not my life. Oh, shit! *(Looking down.)* I'm sorry, I'm trying not to swear. It's hard, you know, to do the right thing, you know.—I'm always asking for forgiveness, because I believe that God understands and he is forgiving, and he knows how hard it is, to do the right thing all the time, even when you want to, more than anything else, and if you fail and you disappoint people, you can just try again, right?

And you can have the intention to try again even while you're failing…failing! I don't suppose there is really any chance of me passing this exam tomorrow. I mean, if I'm going to be punished for this, and I'm sure I will be, that will probably be the punishment, because when you're trying to do the right thing and make people proud of you, Satan wants you to fail. And then you end up being a huge disappointment. Well, if I'm not going to be a doctor, I wonder what I will be?—Maybe I will be a bum!—And Sakina will say, "I can't marry him, he's a BUM!!!" *(He is getting quite worked up at this point as he gets closer to orgasm.)* And I will say, "GOOD!!!! BECAUSE THIS BUM WOULDN'T MARRY YOU WHEN HELL FREEZES OVER!" AND HER PARENTS WILL SAY, "HOW DARE YOU TALK TO OUR DAUGHTER LIKE THAT!!! AND I WILL SAY I JUST DID! ! AND MY PARENTS WILL SAY, "HOW DARE YOU TALK TO HER PARENTS LIKE THAT, YOU ARE A GREAT DISAPPOINTMENT," AND I WILL SAY, "MOM, DAD EAT *(He orgasms.)* SHIIIT!!!!" *(He falls to his knees in shock, and slowly as if almost in slow motion he doubles over on the floor, unconsciously going into the Islamic position of prayer. After a few seconds, he regains his composure and attempts to stand and button up his pants.* Thank you Angel, I mean Kar—…I mean Angel.

Seagull 2000

Dianne Murray

Scene: here and now

Serio-Comic
Boris: a celebrated author. 40s–50s

> *Here, Boris relates the downside of being an author obsessed with recording the minutiae of life for possible future use.*

BORIS: Wait a minute. Are you a reporter in disguise?

[NINA: No. I just like hearing about your life. Other than Irene, I don't know anyone like you. It must be so great. That's all.]

BORIS: I know your enthusiasm is honest, but sometimes it's irritating when people think just because you've accomplished certain things…in my case the novels…that life is sweet. Believe it or not there's a down side. I'm possessed by this never ending gnawing feeling. Or is it a desire? No, desire sounds pleasurable. Yes, it's definitely an annoyance that never goes away. I must record everything I encounter. Say, I meet a person with cocktail sauce in the corner of their mouth; and that strikes me in some way. If I can't write it down right then, which by the way drives me crazy, I make a mental note, and eventually document the facts within a reasonable amount of time so I won't forget. Nina, I must confide that it would be a nice reprieve to just sleep, take a bath or have a normal conversation with an attractive girl without this internal nagging, but then I'm not totally complaining because I never know when I'll need this stuff, when some story requires my special touch. Say when the hunter meets the lion. Maybe he'll recite a prayer, one I heard at a wedding, or maybe he'll tell a joke because he wants to laugh in the face of death. Lucky for me, I jotted one down that I overheard in the men's room. My brain actually hurts because so many ideas are traveling through so fast. I experience constant frustration. Tape-recording isn't fast enough, because the weirdest thing happens between thinking and verbal speech. Too much gets lost. The closest I come to feeling satisfied is with pen in hand and writing like a mad man, because every now and then the pen is right on top of the word. My little surfboard riding the waves of words. The day is coming when we just plug into our brains and watch the thoughts appear on the screen. Then we'll have some crazy stories. Pushing literature into the twenty-first century. The writings will probably scare the crap out of everybody and I can't wait.

Seven Dates with Seven Writers

Paula Kamen

Scene: here and now

Comedic
A. Wright: a pompous screenwriter and playwright. 20–30

> *Here, a nightmare of a blind date drones on mightily about his favorite subject: himself.*

A. WRIGHT: You know, Rhoda, you are so refreshing...I shouldn't be so personal on the first date, but you are so different from so many of the legions of women that A. Wright Rushoff has gone out with. As you might guess, I am constantly meeting all these beautiful and glamorous young actresses. My life is just a virtual parade of nubile starlets, kicky young fillies, offering me their lithe and tender bodies with no strings attached.

And, you wouldn't believe it, but constantly dating and having sex with drop-dead size four women is dull. Yeah, dull. They just bore me with their constant working out, fretting about their appearance, about gaining an ounce or two. But you, you, you! It's so refreshing to go out with someone who obviously doesn't care a bit about their appearance! Who doesn't waste time thinking about working out or being physically fit. You obviously eat whatever you please and don't waste any time exercising......No, that's a compliment!

With you, that lack of physical connection makes our *minds* more free to meet. The stimulation we share is in our cerebral cortex, not our loins. Besides, those nymph starlets don't care about me. They are only making love to the *legend* of A. Wright Rushoff, not to the real, breathing, feeling, multi-dimensional man.

That reminds me, I have something very important to tell you.

Not to get too serious all of a sudden but…I'll tell you…This is kind of embarrassing, to discuss these things so openly…I know that this is our first meeting, but A. Wright was wondering if we could go back to your place afterwards…get some privacy…You see, *(Taking out a massive pile of papers.)* I have my new play here, and I want to give you the opportunity to proofread it for me. When I met you at the workshop, I was most impressed with your grammatical skills. My last girlfriend—she was gorgeous, but she doesn't read much beyond the "Is My Boyfriend Taking Me For Granted Because He Hasn't Bought Me Flowers in Two Weeks?" quiz in Cosmo. And worst of all, she could only type twenty-five words a minute!

…Well, yes. It sounds fascinating because it is fascinating…You'll love the play. I dare even call it an opus. One of my most inspired. An imaginary conversation in Paris between Maimonides, Martin Buber, Einstein, the Virgin Mary and A. Wright Rushoff…You know, surreal metafiction, that's real writing. OK, we'll discuss it later…

Did I tell you how refreshing you are? Oh, there's the waitress. I bet you're going to order dessert! I've never been with a woman who ordered dessert before…

Seven Dates with Seven Writers

Paula Kamen

Scene: here and now

Comedic
Rickie: a self-styled "improvisor." 20–30

> *Rickie's colorful past is something he loves to talk about…and talk about…and talk about…*

RICKIE: *(Delivers this in many different voices and accents.)* Well, I used to write scripts for the theater. Then *(Switching identities.)* I was transformed, BORN AGAIN. *(Does impression of "born again" minister.)* I sllllllided *(Physically slides.)* or fell *(Falls dramatically.)* into an improv group, at the *(Southern drawl.)* Crabass Theater Company, which later evolved, or rather, devolved into the *(Snarling.)* Extreme Irritation players. At that point, everything I had ever seen before seemed fake and fettered *(Overly proper English accent.)* by rules and propriety.

They're a gorilla *(Makes noises like gorilla.)* theater company, you know, challenging the audience with the use of obscenity: every other word was fuckshitassdickcuntblahblahblah. In every show, we have at least a dozen references to anal sex; it's in our mission statement. We actually embrace these "swear words" and tabooed sexual acts, as our building blocks of art. You know, nothing works better than shock—to get people to really look at their sacred cows and re-examine what they hold so dear in their complacent and narrow lives. And, we also have the power of the collective on our side. No tyrannical author. We only improvise everything together, never with any binding, oppressive script…..No, we don't have any rules at all. I meant it. The rules are: there ain't no rules…Yeah, that can be truly liberating, which is the whole point of being an artist. Following formulas is too easy—there ain't no art in it.

You might have heard of our most famous show. Without any script, we all put on an obscene holiday rock opera, "The 69th Day of Christmas," which we improvised on the spot and changed every weekend. In every three-hour show, we actually came up with a good eleven minutes of solid material!

Yeah, that's the only pure way to do it. No prior thought or planning. Real writing is: not writing. Like, my one-man show. I refuse to plan anything. When the curtain opens, I'm up there for two hours with no script. I have the audience give me a title of something, and I just see where it takes me. OK, give me a book title…OK, let's think of something easier. Come on, Rhoda. Come on. Then give me a place…Come on, loosen up! Let those inhibitions go. Shed that repression, that uptightness, that emotional suit of armor that obviously has been holding you prisoner for too long! Yell! Scream! Dance! How 'bout an animal noise? How about a little quack? Or a grunt? Clucking? You must like clucking? A moo, perhaps?

Something Is Wrong

Robert Vivian

Scene: the deck of a house overlooking a vast lake

Dramatic
Lance: a man obsessed with his own obsessions. 52

> *As his wife and brother-in-law lounge on the deck of the lake house, Lance bounces relentlessly between the deck and the kitchen, furious that no one seems to care that he isn't enjoying himself.*

LANCE: Nothing I say makes the slightest difference here. You're ape shit in your rocking chairs. I could tell you I'm going crazy, that I see everything about this that is so horrible, and you'd just shrug and sip with your little pinkie raised. You have a love affair with death. But when you're alive, when you're alive as I am, you can no longer just sit here and admire the view. You simple can't.

[LOUISE: You could once in a while.]

LANCE: Oh, now we're counting pennies, eh? Your problem is you think I exaggerate. But wait a minute. What am I exaggerating? Is it my intelligence I'm exaggerating? No. I don't think so. I'm not that smart. Is it the wind in the trees I'm exaggerating? No. We hear that, too. Then it must be death I'm exaggerating. Yes, that must be the culprit. I'm exaggerating death. I have no choice, do I? I've never been dead so of course I exaggerate the boogey man. I peel grapes for the boogey man, I get on my hands and knees for the boogey man. I say, Please, please, please forget what year it is and let me put it off for one more day, one more week, one more hour. I want to continue scraping by. I want my feet firmly planted in the here and now, I don't want to think about my life, anything but that, who do I pray to at night but myself in another form? We all know how nasty human beings are but I'm different, I have a heart, and I'm scared out of my pants that you're going to throw me over the goat mound. But the truth is, I have nothing to do with any of this. I want a reason.

Spellcheck

Caroline Rosenstone

Scene: a third grade classroom, the first day of school

Serio-Comic
Louis: a man on the edge. 30s–40s

> *Louis has lost his child in a divorce and his job at the univer-sity press. Here, he starts his new career as a third grade teacher with questionable results.*

LOUIS: Here we are, first day. You a little nervous? Yes, you are! It's natural—your first day of third grade. I'm a little nervous, too. It's my first day, too. Being a teacher. I *was* a big cheese editor for Yale Press, but we parted. Different "paths."

I'm meant to be here. So are you. This is a holy exchange. We begin and end, with Truth. Truth Number One? Everybody hates the first day of school. (I just walked in on the school nurse chug-ging down a whole fistful of aspirin. We hope it was aspirin…)

(Louis produces a large bag filled with conch shells, which he hands to members of the audience.) So, I brought us presents! Go on, honey, reach into the bag. Ooo, know what that's called? A *conch* shell.

(Louis acts as if responding to a schoolchild's question.) You want to know how to *sell*…oh, how to *spell* conch shell. C-O-N.… *(Irritated.)* Doesn't matter. I mean, spell it however you'd like.… *(Louis holds a conch shell to his ear, helping a schoolchild to do the same.)* Hear the sea? Hold it…that's right, up to your ear. Everybody gets one! *(Louis hands out more conch shells.)* Take a shell, sweetie. Thank you, *you're* the gift. Everyday at the end of school, we'll hold these to our ears and listen to the sea. Summer hasn't left this class for dead! Here's our number-one rule: Whatever you do in this class is correct. This is a no-fail class. You are perfect.

Look how you smile. What beautiful smiles! See, I was meant to be here; that Yale Press was a hellhole. Dark. Dark as a bat's armpit. But here, we smile. *(In a Tibetan accent.)* The buddha always smile. Those fat little buddha's—smile, smile. *(Louis acts as if responding to another schoolchild's question.)* "What is a buddha?" A very wise person devoted to God, like a minister or priest. *(Louis rolls from behind the desk a large gong, which he sounds, and speaks in a Tibetan accent.)* The sound of the bell bring us back to our true self. *(Louis reacts to a male in the audience as if responding to a schoolboy's challenging question.)* Excuse me? Your mother says "no religion in the schools, it's the law?" Because of "separation of churches over states?" That's "separation of church *and* state," cupcake. What's the big problem here? *(Louis raises his hand, indicating that students may volunteer to answer. None do.)* "Separations" divide things into good and bad, in and out. These ideas kill and maim people and cause domestic vendettas like divorce.

Today is the anniversary of my divorce. My only child taken from me like a sack of groceries delivered to the wrong address. "Life is suffering," the Buddhists say. So: I have *rich* life!

Let's do names! Let's start with you. *(Louis selects an audience member and reacts as if she has told him her name.)* You're "Cleo." Welcome! *(Louis goes to the audience member he used as the challenging boy.)* And you, Mr. "Separation-of-Churches-Over-States?" "Myron." Incredible. Seven years ago your mother looks upon a harmless infant splashing in its bassinet and names it Myron. *(Kindly.)* We're with you, Myron. *(Louis goes to another male in the audience, reacting as if he volunteers his name. This person has been given a lunch-box to hold.)* Now this young man? "Andy?" You said…ANDY? *(To Andy.)* I see. I'm honored.

Open your notebooks, everyone! Our first lesson is automatic writing! Automatic writing means writing without stopping to think, writing whatever you feel…Thus do we break through the barrier of the rational mind to essences. Write, draw, let your hand move of its own accord across the paper. *(Louis moves among the audience as if checking their schoolwork.)* Don't think, just write, scribble…good…excellent!

Let's see… *(Louis goes to a new person to check her paper, reacting as if she offers her name.)* …"Alberta!"…you wrote…a sentence!…about peanut butter! Good! *(Confidentially to Alberta.)* It's very fattening, you know. *(Louis goes to Cleo and checks her paper.)* And Cleo, you've drawn…that's either…um… a cow…or the word "utilitarian!" Brilliant!

Lesson Number Two. Write this down: "Synchronicity." Synchronicity. *(Louis responds with irritation, as if someone has asked him to spell.)* No, I won't spell it, you spell how it *feels* to you. Freewrite, freewrite! *(Louis responds as if a new audience member asks a question and volunteers her name.)* You want to know what "synchronicity" means? Okay…Tashima, say…you're in your psychiatrist's office—it's almost evening, silvery twilight— and just as you say, "My whole life is falling apart," a piece of pottery falls off the bookshelf and breaks into a million pieces. That's "synchronicity."

Or say that one year to the day of the wrenching away of your beloved child, Andy, fate sets you before an entire classroom of beautiful children, one of whom is named Andy. That's synchronicity.

Meaningful coincidences that are signs from God. *God,* Myron, deal with it. Signs from God that we must have faith. We are not bereft. My son is not gone from me. *(Louis goes to Andy.)* His spirit shines through you, Andy, like flame rising from a candle. Is this your lunch box, Andy? Can I play with the lock for a minute? *(Louis responds as if Andy assents and takes his lunch box. To Andy.)* I'm fine now, Andy. When they took you away, I blamed myself. But a man who compromises his standards lives with his face in the dog bowl. We were two peas in a pod, but you were stolen away. Now I'm podless. Without pod. *(Louis returns the lunch box to Andy. To the class.)* How'd we all do automatic-writing on synchronicity? Tashima, you wrote…no, drew!…a …nasturtium? A daisy! Excellent. That's how it felt to you. Cleo, what's this here…this wet spot…you sneezed? Good release of toxins. *(Louis responds as if Myron has made a request.)* Myron, what? You "need it quiet to write." No, you don't. Just keep writing. *(Louis goes to Myron.)* Let's see…That's what you wrote? *That* is how you *feel* it? Try again. It's bad to struggle. *Relax,* okay? *(To Andy.)* Andy, dear…but there's nothing here on your paper. Ah, I see, the blank page is the *void.* Very intuitive and brilliant. (I won't let them take you again. I promise.)

Myron, what's going on over there? You wrote…the same thing! The same thing all over again! Didn't I tell you to try something else? Look what he writes!

Over and over, "synchronicity" spelled "s-y-n-c-h-r-o-n-i-c-i-t-y." Some constructive criticism? It sucks! *(Louis responds to Myron's defense.)* "It's correctly spelled, check the dictionary?" I don't care about dictionaries; dictionaries are the Gestapo! Other people draw daisies and The Void and you give me "correct spelling"? You have a computer at home, Myron? Mmm hmm. I thought so. Do you have Spellcheck on your computer? Mmm hmm. Last year they fired me at Yale Press for my "bad spelling," but I spell however I want to, on principle, and no one—certainly no computer—dicks around with it. Do you have Brush-Your-Teeth-Check on your computer? Going-Out-The-Front-Door-Check? Go-Poopie-Check?

Myron, you will take this note with you down to the principal's office. *(Louis takes a pen and paper from his desk and writes.)* "Dear Mr. Thornton: Myron…? Plotnick is to be assigned to another class, where he may strangle creativity with greater abandon than I allow in my classroom." *(To Myron.)* We're crying, Myron? Good release of toxins. Take this note, wipe your face off with your shirt, say goodbye. *(Louis, waving goodbye, responds as if watching Myron exit.)* Goodbye.

He's gone. Look, Tashima, Cleo, Andy, our beautiful smiles—gone! Crammed down our throats. *(Coughing.)* Get it out. *(Louis takes a bottle of pills from his pocket and shakes a good number into his hand.)* A homeopathic remedy for stress, who wants some? Our beautiful smiles! Andy angel, take one, then pass them around—to Tashima, to Cleo...Just suck 'em up. Aren't they nice?

Myron didn't mean to do harm. He was doing the best he could. Awakening comes slowly. Open your notebooks. Let your hand flow across the page, however you feel it in your soul...freewrite, freewrite, the word "forgiveness." *(Louis picks up a conch shell.)* Oops! That funny Myron left his shell. Who wants Myron's shell? Nobody? *(He puts the shell to his ear.)* Two...piccolos! and a tuba! Stravinsky!

The Steamfitter's Dream

Mark Donnelly

Scene: a bar

Dramatic
Pete: a world-weary alcoholic. 30s–40s

> *Pete's nephew seems to be sliding towards the kind of unhappy life that Pete lives. Here, he does his best to paint a realistic picture of his empty existence for the young man while encouraging him to stay in college.*

PETE: *(Holds up his hands, palms facing Mike.)* See these hands? That's what I got. I got a bum back and my legs are shaky and I'm pushing forty-six. I'm walking up ten flights of stairs on an office building job on the Westside. Drafty as hell. I grab a couple of quick ones at lunch and I rush to the nearest bar at 3:30 when we quit. Lots of days I look out at the sky from way up there on that building and I hold on tight to a steel beam to keep myself from diving off. It'd be easy to make it seem like an accident…walking around up there, unfinished, exposed building…can be a real tightrope walk. Guys could think, "Hey, he tripped on some pipe or boards and over he went. Poor Pete O'Rourke. Sweet guy, lot of fun. We'll miss him." And the laugh of it is I'm afraid of heights. *(Pause.)* Sometimes I hide from the other guys on the job I get so scared inside, and I'm holding on to that steel beam for dear life. Only it ain't bad war memories driving me nuts. It's my life being fucked, a knowing that I can't get through a day without a fucking drink…a bunch of fucking drinks. *(Pause.)* This morning I got to the job early before anyone else, and I was holding on to a beam again, looking out at the sky and it was cloudy and blue…a nice March morning, kind of clear feeling…you can feel the spring coming in after that miserable cold winter…and I asked God up in that heaven to get me through the day so I could go to that hospital sober when I saw my brother. *(Pause.)* If I could cut off my arm to take away his pain, I would. *(Pause.)* But it don't work that way. *(Pause.)* And I looked out to God somewhere out in that sky…the God that I'd stopped talking to a long time ago…it was almost like I could picture him in the clouds, the way they used to show him in paintings in the Catechism books in grammar school…and I asked him to help Jim through this. *(Pause.)* I got less cluttered up there near the sky, like I was closer to God…and I got a little bit of peace…not a whole big peace, but enough for now. And that got me through the morning and I didn't have to have a drink at lunch. And I was OK in the afternoon. *(Pause.)* So I did go sober to see him. You found me in here, sure. But I did have some peace today. And you know what? I'm gonna go back early again tomorrow and talk to that morning sky and try to get a little more peace. *(Pause.)* Maybe someday I'll see my Mom and my Pop out there in those clouds, too, and they could be comfortable somehow together, not having to fight anymore.

Tied Up In Chains

Laura Henry

Scene: Venezuela

Serio-Comic
Saul Manthony Degroup: a devoted missionary. 30–50

> *God has dictated the New Letter for the Next Millennium directly to humble Saul, who here prepares to share the Lord's word with the faithful.*

SAUL MANTHONY DEGROUP: He spoke to me last night. I had my ears open wide for nine years and eleven months and I was plannin on closing them on the anniversary of the decade. But he must have been listening to my thoughts. 'Cause he got right up to the cutoff date and then it happened. He spoke.

The first time it happened I was an ordinary guy. I was sitting on this big rock underneath this big blue sky. Feeling the warm air. Everything so lovely, thinking about Armageddon.

You know Armageddon don't you? The battle in the sky? It's that time when God comes down and fights the evil on our black planet. There's a big rain, drops of blood that feels like fire, but it ain't no pain compared to what we got down here, even on the good days. And there's a song in the air and a big white smoke and we all, the babies and the mothers and the folks who spend their days toilin' on the earth for a dime and no respect, all get wrapped up in the arms of God. And we fly through the air up to him in his heavens laughing and shouting and the Great Chant goes up Arma, Arma, Arma Geddon. Just like that. Arma, Arma, Arma Geddon. And all of us peoples are saved. The earthly peoples, swept up into the sky singing. And we are free at last, free and happy and there is no pain.

I was high up there, that first day, high on the beauty of the rapture of my thoughts when it happened. Oh, no. He didn't speak to me yet. Not yet. But I heard the break bell clanging, and it was time to go back to work again.

And right there, coming through the noise of the break bell was when it started, a strange sound. A small sound at first, a little hum, so tiny at the start that I didn't even notice. I stood up, and it got a little louder, and as I walked back towards the shop, the noise shaped itself into sounds that began to shape themselves into words and then suddenly I could hear the words. A voice from nowhere talking to me loud and clearlike.

The voice said, "Saul Manthoney Degroup, I am talking to you." I knew the voice. It stopped me in my tracks, But I said, "Who are you?" just to check. And then He spoke. And he said, "It is me. The Great One. And Saul Manthoney, just like the Saul before you, I have come calling." I couldn't believe it. I said, "God?" And he said, "It is me" and I said, "I'm gonna be late to work. Do you realize that? I've been sittin here on a bench thinking about you through my whole lunch hour and now it's over and now you want to talk." And he said, "Yes, Saul Manthoney. I don't always call at the most convenient time."

When God speaks to you, you don't tell him He'll have to wait. You sit back down and you listen. And that's exactly what I did. I put my butt back down and got ready to receive His word. And He said to me, "Saul, you've got things to do. You go to work now. That is what you should do. But keep your ears open to me. Keep those ears in your heart open. Because I'm coming back. You are my blessed child. I am choosing you to spread my word in Venezuela." And then he left again. Just like that.

So I went to work, but I'm sayin' right now, I couldn't keep a clear head. I just kept thinking, "Jesus is coming. Jesus is coming to me, Saul Manthoney, just like he came to the other Saul. He's calling to me." I felt more special inside then than I ever felt in my entire life.

When I got home I cleaned the place. I put on a nice shirt and my good shoes. I combed my hair neat and settled down, ready to receive God's word. He was late. I couldn't help but watch the clock. Eight thirty, nine, nine forty-five…I read my Bible, clock hands still moving. I took a walk. I sang. It got later. No voice. I stayed up through the night, listening and praying. Two-thirty, two forty-five, three and work in the morning still to come. But He didn't come back. Maybe He just got too busy, I thought. Maybe he was too busy for a man like me. And then I remembered, he didn't say when he was coming back, he just said to keep my ears open. Maybe he wasn't coming back for a while. Maybe there was something I had to learn first, a test, to prove myself. And I thought of the other part of what he said. I was sent to spread his word in Venezuela. Venezuela? I knew I had to follow Him, so I left all my earthly possessions, cashed in all the money I had in the world and picked up and went to Venezuela on a plane through the night.

How I got to Venezuela is another story. We don't have time for that one. You're here to receive God's new letter for the Next Millennium. I'm holding it right here in my hands. God gave it to me and now I am here to give it to you. It is my greatest mission in life.

I've been here ten years, to the day. It wasn't easy at first. I didn't have any money, no place to go. I didn't even know how to speak right. Ohee, I was scared when I came here. Boy, was I scared. But God always has us in his hands and he took care of me and slowly, I learnt to say what I needed to say and I ended up in this place along the Rio Orinico and was taken in by some nice folks. I told them my story, that God had sent me, and they let me stay there so I could tell stories for God, just the way I'm telling you today. And soon I was going all over to tell my stories and people were coming from all over to hear them. They wanted to receive joy. And they seemed to get it.

But I can tell you now that the whole time I was preaching like a called man, I felt like a fake. A crazy man singing about Armageddon and the word of God. 'Cause God never spoke to me again. These last ten years, I've been waiting with my ears open and my heart wide, singing the praises of God. And He never again let me receive His word. Not like the first time.

Was I a fake? I didn't know. I would plead with him and

plead with him. God, I'd pray, give me a sign. Let me know you're here, that I'm not some crazy man in a new land with a grand delusion. Let me know you sent me here. Still, no word. And I kept preachin' and talkin', telling people about the word of God, but all the time, doubting bigger than Thomas. Am I a fake? If I'm not why won't you come back? Please, please come back. Still, no word.

Until last night. There I was, an ordinary man on an ordinary day. I'd finished my preaching for the night and had just stepped into the bathtub, ready to take myself a hot shower and the water was on, streaming down me, and I was singing songs as loud as I could when I heard this still small voice that I recalled from those other days. Soft at first, but this time I knew for sure what it was. I stopped. "God?" I said? "It is me, my son," he said back. "God," I said, "Can't you see I'm in the shower?" He laughed and said, "Saul, my child. I love you. I'll come back at a better time." "Oh, no you don't," I said. "You said that last time and I've been waitin' for ten whole years. I'll be danged if I'm gonna miss you cause I'm taking a bath. Talk to me. Talk to me now." And he said, "But Saul, you're all wet. I'm going to need you to be ready with a piece of paper. You're going to take dictation for me. You're going to write a letter that will beat the great letters of Paul." To miss this chance, what a fool I would have been.

I'm ready, God. I'm ready right now. And I stepped out of the shower, all soaped up and everything and I put a towel around my middle and I found some paper and I sat my butt down on the chair and I waited for him to speak again. And you know what? He waited for me too. For me. Saul Manthoney Degroup. He waited until I was situated and then he began to speak again. It came in spurts. I'd listen, he'd say a little. I'd write. He'd say a little more, I'd write. I didn't question a thing, just wrote it down, wrote down every word he said. It took all night. I'm a little tired now, if I must say so myself. It's a rough job, being secretary for the Lord. But now I got it—my letter—just as inspired as the letters from Paul, and I have come here to read it to you today.

At first I was a little nervous. I read it over just a few minutes ago, you see, and I know that some of what I have to say to you might seem a little crazy. I can't help it. I didn't come up with the idea. It's all God's thoughts. I just held the pen. So don't judge, if you start to feel like the words come out a little bit strange. Hold on till the end of the message. It is God's great message to me and to you, my friends. The answer to all our prayers, everything we've been waiting for since the last letters from Him. It's the New Letter for the Next Millennium. Hold on to your seats. Close your eyes. Open your hearts. Get ready to receive his word. *(Saul takes hold of his letter and begins to speak.)* Dear friends: Kiss someone you love when you receive this letter. With love all things are possible. *(He stops suddenly.)* Wait a second. *(He listens.)* I hear His voice again. *(Saul listens intently. Then he begins to have a conversation with God.)* What? Are you sure? But we worked on it all night…But Lord, it is so beautiful and these people have come today to hear your word…I understand, but…But…Wait…Don't leave me like this…Goodbye. Goodbye. *(He folds the paper up and looks sadly at the audience.)* I'm very sorry. I thought he wanted me to share his words with you today. That's why I rang the bell and asked you all to come. But it was my mistake. A misunderstanding, really. I just didn't…This letter that we worked so hard on last night, this perfect specimen of God's word…He says it is not time yet. It's a letter for the new millennium, He says and the new millennium just hasn't come yet. *(Saul looks out at the people.)* I guess you can all go home. I'm very sorry.

Don't despair. Keep your hearts and your ears open, God said to tell you that. His word will be known. Be ready when the time comes. But first there is much work for me to do.

He says I have to translate it into English immediately and send it to the people back home. He says the folks there need his message more than anything. But we in Venezuela will receive it too. Be ready for the day it comes. Be open to it.

You must leave now. I wish I could have read you the letter but I must obey God. I have to. You do understand, don't you? I have work to do. So much translation…and I have to finish my bath. The soap is beginning to itch.

   (*Lights go down on him.*)

'Til the Rapture Comes

Edward Napier

Serio-Comic

Ian Walker: a young boy with some unusual problems. 11

> *Ian's mom, a skilled nurse, is addicted to prescription med-*
> *ication. Ian has turned to God in a effort to cope with his dif-*
> *ficult home life and burgeoning hormonal urges. Here, Ian*
> *prays on his way home from school.*

IAN: Lord, in the Apostle Paul's, "First Epistle to the Thessalonians," he tells us to pray without ceasing. But when I try to pray during class, Lord, I don't pay as close attention as I should, so I stopped, and I apologize for that. But I know I'm not supposed to ask for anything until I've confessed all my sins, so: Dear Lord Jesus Christ, today, I got a hardon, and I know, that's a sin—I suppose, I should say erection to you, Lord Jesus, because that's more polite, and my hardon lasted so long, I thought it would never go away—all through Science—because I kept thinkin' about lying on top of Stacy Robertson without no clothes, and I know that's a sin, and the more I tried not to think about it, the more clear the pictures became in my mind, because Lord, she has boobs, and she has the third largest boobs of any girl in sixth grade. And my erection did not go away until I had to stand up in front of the class and give my report on Sir Isaac Newton's, "Laws of Motion." And I felt the sin of pride when I gave my report, Lord, because I showed a genuine picture of Newton from out of our *Encyclopedia Britannica* at home, and all the kids thought that was cool, so I went from the sin of lust to the sin of pride, Lord, and no sooner had I sat down at my desk, but that Bucky Ramey called me a faggot, and I told him that his Daddy was mentally retarded—even though it's true, Lord, his Dad's very stupid and has a terrible speech impediment, and his brother, Gooby Ramey, got caught screwin' Flossie Maynard's heifer, so Lord, I just went

123

from sin to sin to not turnin' the other cheek which is also a sin in less than ten minutes! I can't stop sinnin', Lord! But I sure try. Oh, purify my heart, Lord Jesus Christ. And Lord, you know, sometimes, I dream I'm on television, and I know that's a sin, because you don't like famous people unless they're famous because of you, and then, I think, well, if I could just be Oral Roberts? And I wonder if that's a sin—to want to be a person I ain't?! So please, forgive me of those sins, and all of the thousands of sins that I commit each and every day that I don't even know are sins. And thank you, Lord, for allowing Petunia to stay with us while my Dad's down in Mingo County. Blessed Jesus, you know, now, this is the third day in a row that my Dad has been gone, and my Mother's takin' off sick leave. Because she's too depressed to go out to that V.A. Hospital and watch 'em die, she says, but I know it's because my Dad's away, because he left mad, because my Mother should understand that a man has to go away on business every now and then. Otherwise, my Daddy wouldn't be the most respected lawyer in our whole County. And he called from Williamson last night to say he wouldn't be home until Thursday evening—which is just tomorrow evening, and she passed the phone to me and wouldn't say good-bye. But Mother hasn't taken any of her sleeping pills in two whole days, Lord. She told me she was going to stop. And I pray that you give her the strength to stop taking drugs, and if there is any way I could be or could act that would keep her from goin' back to 'em, please reveal it to me. Because I want my Mother and Dad to get along like Stacy Robertson's parents do. And please, don't let my Mother die. Please, keep her off drugs and don't let her die. Please, don't let her die, Lord. And I ask you to please, please be with her when I come home. Amen, Lord. Amen.

'Til the Rapture Comes

Edward Napier

Dramatic
Wilbur: a long-suffering husband. 50s

> *Wilbur has learned to live with his wife's addiction to pre-*
> *scription medication. Here he tries to explain to his oldest son*
> *why she'll never stop.*

WILBUR: Son, I asked your Mother's psychiatrist, Dr. Hubbard, not to prescribe your Mother any more of those goddam sleeping pills. I told him that I believed that she had developed a dependency on them. He assured me she had not, but that he would not prescribe her anymore. So then she started getting her friend, Dr. Watts, to issue a prescription for them. So now, she has another source. And I strongly believe if she didn't get them from Doc Watts or some other doctor, that she'd have me out on street corners pursuing dope peddlers, so that she could get herself a fix.

[WILLY: Well, Dad, it's wake up time. What can I say?]

WILBUR: Two or three times a year, she'll go for a couple or three days without taking the damn things, and I can not tell you how I hope that this is it: It's over. But no. Never. Never is.

[WILLY: You should commit her to the goddamn insane asylum is what you should do.]

WILBUR: Son, I couldn't have your Mother committed to the insane asylum.

[WILLY: Why not? She's crazy!]

WILBUR: I know she's crazy, but she knows what the capitol of the United States is—that she lives in the state of West Virginia—that that goddam half-witted-should-have-burned-the-tapes-destroyer-of-the-Republican-party Nixon is President. That it is 1974. Yes, Sir. Your Mother could pass any kind of competency test they'd ever want to give her. And when she insisted that we go up to

125

the Cleveland Clinic last year to have complete physical examina-
tions—she was looking for any doctor who might corroborate
her preposterous self-diagnosis of yet another of those obscure
terminal illnesses she'd come across in her Merk Manual—and as
soon as we arrived, we were filling out the basic medical history
questionnaires, and we came to the question, have you taken any
prescribed medication in the past six months, and she wrote, no.
And I said, "Althea Dale, are you not going to inform these people that you have taken just about every type of barbiturate and
painkiller legally available in the United States every day of your
life for the past six and a half years, and she said, "You go to hell
you son-of-a-bitch. If I ever hear you say anything like that, again,
I'll divorce you. And I'll take everything you've got."

   [WILLY: God.]

WILBUR: Such a shame.

   [WILLY: I don't understand how it is she keeps her job.]

WILBUR: They say she is an excellent nurse.

To Have and To Hold

Paul Harris

Scene: NYC

Serio-Comic
Michael: a philosophical drag queen. 20–30

> *When asked by a gay comedian how he got his start in drag,*
> *Michael tells the following story.*

MICHAEL: I don't know exactly how it started. That's a lie. It was a Halloween party. I was eighteen and I decided that I would go as a woman. I was dating this girl at the time and she helped with it. I remember going out to buy a dress and make-up and things and I would say "I need a dress for my girlfriend. She's…She's about my size." That's how I found out that I was a 'twelve!' I felt very strange at first. But you know the first time that I put make-up on at home in my bathroom—with the door locked—and put on a dress I suddenly felt as if I was someone else. My girlfriend thought it was all a joke for this party. But I knew it wasn't. I liked it. I went out walking down the street and I passed. No heads turned. And believe me in Akron, Ohio if anyone had suspected that I was a man—heads would have turned! I always remember some advice my Mother gave my sisters about jewelry. "When you think you've got enough on—take one piece off." It was good advice. Bad drag queens always wear too much jewelry. They wind up looking like Christmas trees.

[JIM: If you meet someone, how do they react?]

MICHAEL: Well, when I moved to New York and 'came out' and started seeing men, dating guys was difficult. I used to put all my gowns and wigs away in a closet and closed the door so that if I ever brought a guy back here he wouldn't see them. I had to work out whether it was someone whom I was likely to see again or not before I told them I did drag. Some gay men are very bigoted, you know. They can't stand drag, I think it challenges their masculinity, or something. Mind you they are the ones who normally want you to screw them into the headboard.

[JIM: Really.]

MICHAEL: I like the element of deception. At work they haven't got a clue. I wouldn't dare say a word. They're very straight. They wouldn't understand. Mind you, I'm not sure that I understand totally. I'm very happy being a man. I mean I don't want to have my dick chopped off and get breasts and things. I like being a man far too much. I love my dick! We should order.

To Have and To Hold

Paul Harris

Scene: NYC

Serio-Comic
Michael: a philosophical drag queen. 20–30

> *Michael here reveals his unique insight into the complex
> woman who was Marilyn Monroe, who has become much
> more than just a drag persona for him.*

MICHAEL: Do you know there are over eighty books about Marilyn
Monroe? I haven't read every one of them but I've read a lot of
them. Do you know that after she had been married and divorced
for three times and everyone fell in love with her she was still very
insecure. She used to go out to some place on Third Avenue in
Midtown wearing a black wig just to see if she could pick someone up. Very often she got found out and some lawyer or
accountant would have a story he would tell for years about the
day he chatted up Marilyn Monroe in a steak house on Third
Avenue. And if ever she came home and no one had tried to chat
her up she would be upset. She always needed to have approval.
I'm afraid I'm a bit like that. I need to be told I'm okay. Why, I
don't know, but I do. I wish I didn't. I've always felt I've had to
fight for affection. It's never been very easy. Drag's been a great
way of hiding. I know it sounds a silly thing to say but it's true.
When you're in drag people forget there's a man in there some-
where. With Marilyn people forgot that inside that body there
was a person. The movie that everyone always goes on about is
"Some Like It Hot." 1959. Everyone loved it. The audiences. The
critics. Arthur Miller, who she was married to at the time. But she
hated it because people said that no one had ever played a dumb
blonde more perfectly. She said, "I've ruined everything for
myself! I'm a dumb blonde forever now." She even had a row
with Arthur Miller about the film because she felt that she looked

like a fat pig. A freak She was fed up with being dumb. She blamed Arthur Miller for letting her make some of her mistakes like playing the dumb blonde in "Bus Stop" and letting Olivier make fun of her. She desperately wanted to be proud of being who she was. I think I'm like Marilyn in some ways. I was never very good at relationships. I lived with someone once. He was Indian—Indrajit, "conqueror of the skies." The relationship was slowly going from bad to worse. It wasn't much of a relationship—we had three weeks of great sex followed by an agreement to bicker for two years. I cared for him though. I had been working on a film as an extra doing night-shots. It was a crappy film. You know an independent movie. And we were all supposed to get paid when they got a distributor. Ha! Fucking, ha! Well, I came home one night soon after dawn. It was about half past six. No sooner had I opened the door when he, Indra, came out of the bedroom fully clothed. He was furious. He accused me of having been unfaithful to him. I hadn't been—well, not that time anyway—but it didn't stop him thinking I had. I was absolutely shattered and tired. I told him to sit down and think it over before he did anything rash, but that if he walked out that was that. In the meantime I went to the bedroom. I lay on top of the bed fully clothed, listening. After about five minutes I heard the front door open and he left. (Pause.) We didn't see each other for years. I mean, we ran into each other but never so we could talk. Then I decided to move. I called him up and told him and said that I thought it would be nice if we met up for dinner. He agreed. Well, we went to this Polish restaurant, Zamoyski's—everything was potatoes and cabbage. Every ounce of my body wanted to rip him to shreds but I didn't. We had the appetizer and the main course but then over dessert I couldn't resist it. I said, "You know Indra when you walked out I was convinced that you were going to come back to me." There was a sudden chill over the table. Then he said, "When I walked out I was convinced that you were going to come after me and ask me to come back." We just sat there looking at each other. I told my Mom. She said, "Well, can't you two get back together again." I said, "No. Don't be silly." Five years had passed.

Unbroken

Sol B. River

Scene: darkness

Dramatic

Man: on a journey towards wisdom and understanding, 20–30

> *Love and lust intertwine in this stream-of-consciousness expression of passion.*

MALE VO: Watch mi, man nu dead, no call im duppy, come here sweet bring de punni come on resist me don't flex de face-ty firs come here and bear me a pickney A my women dat, mi nu want fi abuse or use, but de love disorder have de controller, as if me is predestine to be a failure, my history disagree becau it deal wid royalty, but de social situation condones de frustration an I wallow in de damnation of myself. Mi love you you know, watch mi nuf gal but I going seccle. Sen it dem glorious pussy coming like dirt to royalty, mi han full can't manage numbers long like lottery, caramel, cream, plain chocolate an dem brownin tings from one to another like being in Narnia. Mi's a don wearing Gucci an Armani dollars falling out de mercede. Start it! Watch mi! smile an stride big up mi pride, ego going flow, ladies from head to toe, inspiration coming like desire, lower parts on fire, can't hold back de addiction for de duration falling into de casket every promise fit, juices like Niagara, flowing like Dunn's river. Kisses sweeter than a Rolex, to your body mines has to flex. Start dem! She loves, I can't spell it, break her heart, you want mi fi regret it? Mi want dat boopsie, when she smile in your eye then come de demise, the man in de moon is smiling im no what I is tinking, speedy love, fast love, bus a nut, come an love, then get back before she attach, like strap to mi back, want to seccle but de psychological babble riding on Robert Palmers saddle, addicted to love, like some hard drug, decease don't bother mi, daze an con-

131

fuse me mus be bemuse, like dem string in a orchestra I'll con-
tinually play her, watch mi, crave mi, desire mi, want mi, carnal
mi, stop mi, hold mi, lust mi, nu badda hide from mi all I want is
yu…crazy mi, irate mi, lunatic mi, demented mi, eh! a wa du yu
is bandooloo? Bob an weave an de women still want me,
buguyaga don't come straight Gaad at me gate but me still nu
fraid. Devil await mi life gwaan speedy, cu-ya telling don dat hell
looks on. Watch mi!

What More?

Mark Blickley

Scene: Iago's exile

Dramatic
Iago: a man who wants to come home. 50–60

> *Here, Iago pleads to be allowed to return to Venice and that his good name be restored.*

IAGO: What tremendous thing am I asking of you and the Signiory? The right to return to my own land so I can plant these old and faithful bones into the soil that I repeatedly risked my life for? Am I asking too much not to have the forming of my name on the lips of the unborn to be a bitter and repulsive utterance for them? I am entering the end of my life. I beseech you, why, when I can almost lick the milkless breast of eternity, would I be so bold as to expose a most indiscriminate vulnerability if what I have offered you are the words and actions of a murderous liar? What will I profit, except to go to my death, my weary extinction, confidently cuddled within the soothing embrace of justice? I am not a monster. Like the Greek heroes before me, I believe that immortality consists of the generational remembrances of greatness that a man has left behind. I do not want this Moor, or his lying wife, or my own betrothed whore to dishonor the magnificence that others, the great and small alike, once openly acknowledged and praised, the jewel once famed and named Honest Iago!

What More?

Mark Blickley

Scene: Iago's exile

Dramatic
Iago: a man who wants to come home. 50–60

Here, bitter Iago denounces Desdemona as a liar.

IAGO: Desdemona is a liar, confirmable by more than just my indictment. As she lay dying, did she not confess to my own wife that Othello did not murder her? What type of woman, prostrate at the feet of eternity, would end her existence by trying to conceal by deceit the most heinous crime imaginable, cold blooded murder? Yet I am the one who emerges from this whole putrid affair as the greatest liar who has ever drawn breath. Believe you me, my last breaths on this earth will not be a plethora of lies, protecting evil. This innocent woman, as you so sweetly refer to her, deceived her own father and lied to her husband about the whereabouts of the satanic handkerchief he presented to her. Scoff at black magic, my friend? Sweet Desdemona died as a result of that enchanted cloth, do not forget that. Yet her unnatural death appeared quite natural to me.

[INTERLOCUTOR: That is a bold and rather cynical statement.]

IAGO: My truthful thoughts on the matter have labeled me a monster instead of the philosopher that I am. Erase the portraits of the noble Moor and the beautiful Desdemona from your mind and you'll understand how this coupling was doomed to failure. It was a battlefield of opposites, two powerful and strong-willed armies out to destroy each other. Youth versus mature age, white skin versus black skin, innocence versus experience, an intensely feminine nature against a masculine extreme, the old civilization of Venice set against the barbaric world of deserts, caverns, and burning suns. Once the moisture clinging to their perfumed sheets evaporated, could any knave not have predicted the circumvent outcome? Cruel, cruel Fate that under the guise of romantic betrayal allows Othello and Desdemona to become the patron saints of thwarted love. While I, Honest Iago, burdened by the same vicious Fate that makes my name a hate-filled mockery, will die alone.

The Widowmaker

Kristan Ryan Donaghey

Scene: an infant ICU

Dramatic
Jack: a desperate new father. 30–40

> *Jack's daughter has been born prematurely with severe prob-
> lems. When Death arrives in the ICU to take her soul, Jack
> instantly recognizes him from his days in Vietnam. Here, Jack
> remembers how he first got to know Death.*

JACK: *(To himself.)* I joined the Army because I wanted to serve my
country and save the oppressed. I never went along with Jane
Fonda and her crowd, but I know they were standing for what
they believed in. We were dying over there for the right to stand
for what you believed in, the right to live in a free country. I was
in the 101st Airborne. We called ourselves the Widowmakers.
The first day I was there, we humped thirty miles through jungle,
ass deep in mud, burned off leeches and slugged through
swarms of bugs I'd never seen before. I passed out in the first ten
miles, my skin on fire like the sun had cut clean through to the
bone. My buddies had to tear open my shirt and pour water over
my chest. I thought DEATH was gonna take me right there on
that mound of leaves and jungle vines. When I came to, everybody was standing around smoking butts, some sipping water
from canteens, the medic nursing me same as a newborn baby.

> [DEATH: *(Laughing.)* Near the end of your tour, that was when
> you met the Bugman.]

JACK: He was a new recruit, cherry. The Bugman had a degree
from Alabama in entomology. We called him the Bugman
because he wrote the name of every bug in Vietnam on his hel-
met. He was my best friend until he got his head blown off in a
firefight two days before I was scheduled to go home. I was sorry

to see that happen. I had to write a letter to his parents. *(Wiping his eyes.)* I didn't even know his parents. I doubt that they'd heard of me before that terrible day when they got my letter.

> [DEATH: You two were such babies, screaming for God when the sky was lit up with fire.]

JACK: *(To himself.)* I wouldn't have called myself a religious man back then but I suppose we all got religion at one minute or another. You couldn't help but find yourself screaming for salvation in the middle of napalm showers. Shit, from day one the jungles sat hunched around us like snakes waiting for rats to come out of their holes. I can still smell the dampness and the smoke of burned out Buddhist temples, still see vines climbing through doors that once stood as honorable as a preacher's podium. Maybe it was the ugliness of DEATH that scratched me, that rose up like a passel of devils wailing in the night. Remembering fills the air around me with the stench of the dead and dying. Jungles and the dead smell the same to me now.

Permissions
Acknowledgments

NOTE: These monologues are intended to be used for audition and class study; permission is not required to use the material for those purposes. However, if there is a paid performance of any of the monologues included in this book, please refer to these permissions acknowledgment pages to locate the source who can grant permission for public performance.

turing, public reading, radio broadcasting, television, video or sound recording, all other forms of mechanical or electronic reproduction, such as CD-ROM, CD-1, information storage and retrieval systems and photocopying, and the rights of translation into foreign languages, are strictly reserved. Particular emphasis is laid upon the matter of readings, permission for which must be obtained from the author's agent in writing. Reprinted by permission of the Dramatists Play Service. Contact: Dramatists Play Service, 440 Park Avenue South, New York, NY 10016. No professional or non-professional production of the play may be given without obtaining, in advance, the written permission of Dramatists Play Service, Inc. and paying the requisite fee. Inqueries regarding all other rights should be addressed to Gil Parker, William Morris Agency, 1325 Ave. of the Americas, New York, NY 10019.

The Crustacean Waltz Copyright © 1998 R. Thompson Ritchie. Reprinted by permission of the author. Contact: Stafford D. Ritchie, 300 Pearl Street Suite 200, Buffalo, NY 14202

Daddy's Heart Copyright © 1998 by Nannette Stone. All rights reserved. Reprinted by permission of the author. Contact: Nannette Stone, Box 789, Holmes, NY 12564

Dating Dummies Copyright © 1998 by Elizabeth Ruiz. Reprinted by permission of the author. Contact: Elizabeth Ruiz, 416 West 47th Street, 2B, New York, NY 10036.

The Dead Boy Copyright © 1998 by Andrew C. Ordover. All Rights Reserved. Reprinted by permission of the author. Contact: Andrew C. Ordover, 381 1st Street, Brooklyn, NY 11215-1905, (718) 369-1766

Dog Copyright © 1998 by Molly Louise Shepard. Reprinted by permission of the author. Contact: Molly Louise Shepard, 822 North Clinton Avenue, Dallas, TX 75208, (214) 942-5994

The Dreamers Copyright © 1998 by Christina Harley. Reprinted by permission of the author. Contact: Christina Harley, 1200 North June Street, #511, Los Angeles, CA 90038, (323) 462-6422

Dutch Treat Copyright © 1998 by Martha King De Silva. Reprinted by permission of the author. Contact: Martha King De Silva, 3456 Newark Street NW, Washington, DC 20016

The Dying Gaul Copyright © 1998 by Craig Lucas. CAUTION: Professionals and amateurs are hereby warned that performance of *The Dying Gaul* by Craig Lucas is subject to royalty. It is fully protected under the copyright laws of the United States of America, and of all countries covered by the International Copyright Union (including the Dominion of Canada and the rest of the British Commonwealth), and of all countries covered by the Pan-American Copyright Convention and the Universal Copyright Convention, the Berne Convention and of all countries with which the United States has reciprocal copyright relations. All rights, including professional, amateur/motion picture stage rights, recitation, lecturing, public reading, radio broadcasting, television, video or sound recording, all other forms of mechanical or electronic reproduction, such as CD-ROM, CD-1, information storage and retrieval systems and photocopying, and the rights of translation into foreign languages, are strictly reserved. Particular emphasis is laid upon the matter of readings, permission for which must be obtained from the author's agent in writing. Reprinted by permission of The William Morris Agency. Contact: Peter Franklin—Author's Agent, William Morris Agency, 1325 Avenue of the Americas, New York, NY 10019, Attn: George Lane, Author's Agent

The Engagement Copyright © 1998 by Richard Vetere. CAUTION: Professionals and amateurs are hereby warned that performance of *The Engagement* by Richard Vetere is subject to royalty. It is fully protected under the copyright laws of the United States of America, and of all countries covered by the International Copyright Union (including the Dominion of

139